FULFILLING THE MISSION

Jesus' Principles for Fulfilling the Mission

ROBERTO HODGSON

Making Christlike disciples in the nations

"The Spirit of the Lord is on me, because he has anointed me to proclaim good news to the poor. He has sent me to proclaim freedom for the prisoners and recovery of sight for the blind, to set the oppressed free, to proclaim the year of the Lord's favor."
(Luke 4:18-19, NIV)

Published by
Casa Nazarena de Publicaciones USA/Canada
Lenexa, Kansas (USA)

Fulfilling the Mission
by Roberto Hodgson

Copyright © 2016
Casa Nazarena de Publicaciones
All Rights Reserved

ISBN: 978-1-56344-026-7

Translation: Edith P. Medley

All Scripture quotations not otherwise designated are from the Holy Bible, *New International Version®, NIV®* Copyright © 1973, 1978, 1984, 2011 by Biblica, Inc.® Used by permission. All rights reserved worldwide.

05/2016

CONTENTS

    About the Author 5
    Dedication 7
    Acknowledgements 9
    Preface 13
    Introduction 17
1. God's Plan 19
2. The Holy Spirit 25
3. The Scriptures 35
4. The Intimate Relationship with the Father 41
5. Prayer and Fasting 47
6. The Election of the apostles 55
7. Preaching and the Movement of the Kingdom of God 63
8. Vision 73
9. Faith 81
10. Compassion 89
11. Organization 95
12. Rest and Spiritual Retreat 103
13. The Servant and Humility 109
14. The Cost of Serving 115
15. Kingdom Fruit 123
16. The Mission Commandment 129
    Conclusion 135
    Notes 137

ABOUT THE AUTHOR

Dr. Roberto Hodsgon graduated in 1985 from Seminario Nazareno de las Americas in Costa Rica with a Bachelor's degree in theology. During his time as a seminarian, he pastored the Church of the Nazarene in San Pedro de Poás from 1982-1985. He was ordained in 1986. He then pastored the Hispanic Church of the Nazarene in Washington, D.C. from 1986-2002. He served as the coordinator of Hispanic Ministries on the Washington D.C. District from 1993-2002.

He completed a Master's degree in theology at Wesley Theological Seminary in Washington, D.C. In 2003 he received the Doctor of Ministry degree from the Graduate Theological Foundation.

Since 2002, he has served as Director of Hispanic Ministries for the USA/Canada Region. He was district superintendent of the Southwest Latin American District from 2007-2012. In May 2012 he was appointed as Director of Multicultural Ministries USA/Canada, a ministry in which he presently serves.

DEDICATION

This book is dedicated to the servants of God for their faithful obedience in the fulfillment of the mission of the Church, "To make Christlike disciples in the nations," especially to those men and women called to shepherd God's flock.

> 1 PETER 5:1-4 *"To the elders among you, I appeal as a fellow elder and a witness of Christ's sufferings who also will share in the glory to be revealed: Be shepherds of God's flock that is under your care, watching over them— not because you must, but because you are willing, as God wants you to be; not pursuing dishonest gain, but eager to serve; not lording it over those entrusted to you, but being examples to the flock. And when the Chief Shepherd appears, you will receive the crown of glory that will never fade away."*

I so appreciate the dedication and effort of our pastors and their families. A very special recognition to those who are bi-vocational. With admiration, I ask: How do you do it? With so many responsibilities, family, ministry, secular work, ministerial studies, etc.! My respects to all of you.

ACKNOWLEDGEMENTS

My deep gratitude to the God of love for his mercy on me, for saving my soul through the merits of his Son Jesus Christ, for purifying my heart with his Holy Spirit, and for calling me to participate in his mission.

To the global Church of the Nazarene for giving me the opportunity to collaborate and serve in the ministry for more than 30 years.

In particular, thanks to Dr. Bob Broadbooks, Regional Director of USA/Canada, for granting me six weeks away from the routine of the office to devote time to write this book.

Finally, to Rev. José Pacheco for putting his masterful touch of experience as an editor to this project.

This book, *Fulfilling the Mission*—*Jesus' Principles for Fulfilling the Mission,* will help pastors and congregations establish balance when the pressures and confusions of the "winds of doctrines" blow around them as they minister. Apostles, such as Paul, warned the churches and the pastors of their time to "watch out for those who cause divisions and put obstacles in your way. ... By smooth talk and flattery they deceive the minds of naive people" because they did not preach Christ. Here, and with an abundance of biblical references, Dr. Hodgson has deposited this work in our hands so that—as expressed in the introduction—we can receive systematic direction via the Scriptures and for the proper fulfillment of the mission of the church following in the footsteps of the Master. As a pastor, I welcome this significant contribution to my life and ministry.

—*Dr. Mario Zani*
Hispanic Pastor of Lenexa Central Church
and Coordinator of Literature, USA/Canada CNP Multicultural

Nobody is better than Dr. Roberto Hodgson, with his vast experience, to write a book like this. He is inspirational and excellent in sharing with small groups and excellent in moving a church with a specific methodology to fulfill the mission of our Lord Jesus Christ. This book is excellent for pastors who are just beginning their ministry or for those who have lost the approach, since this book reflects a comprehensive and balanced ministry of prayer, vision, preaching, teaching, development of leaders, rest, and character development—all of which are necessary for an enduring ministry.

—*Rev. Rigoberto Acosta*
Director of Hispanic Ministries, District of Virginia

With his practical, simple, and direct style, Dr. Roberto Hodgson has prepared a necessary "check list" for all of us in the ministry. Whether you are receiving the call anew, experiencing a difficult moment, are on the verge of collapse, or even if you are doing very well in the fulfillment of the mission, stop! Carefully review these principles established by the divine Master and you will get renewed strength, renewed vision and a fresh anointing to continue to "finish the race and complete the task the Lord Jesus has given" (Acts 20:24).

—*Rev. Obed Jáuregui*
Pastor, Bethany Church of the Nazarene, Miami, Florida

Jesus' Principles for Fulfilling the Mission is a fluid, direct and simple resource for teaching and doing Jesus' mission. Dr. Hodgson gathers the key teaching elements and shows us how to do it in accordance with the wise advice of Jethro to Moses in Exodus 18:20. I recommend this book to every believer as a valuable help and resource in our missional work.

—*Pedro Julio Fernandez*
Pastor, Emanuel Church of the Nazarene,
Toronto, Ontario, Canada

Fulfilling the Mission is a biblically centered and theologically correct book practical in its nature. Dr. Hodgson expresses in a simple, practical, and clear way the why, how, and cost of fulfilling the mission. This book will inspire the experienced pastor, instruct the young pastor, and help the local leader who desires to become an effective contributor in service to God. *Fulfilling the Mission* will be a positive addition to the library of any Christian leader.

—*Dr. Orlando Serrano*
District Superintendent, Western Latin American District V

PREFACE

For several years I have been critical of the way in which many Christians approach their missionary responsibility. Sometimes we have good, beautiful, and sound doctrines and administrative principles as well as a lovely infrastructure in place to develop a healthy church, but we fall short when we want to apply the holistic and missional life of Jesus as a contextual and practical model in the life of the church.

I have discovered, as have thousands of other servants of God, that if the church wishes to be salt and light as Jesus said in Matthew 5:13-14, it not only requires solid and abundant arguments, but also, I believe, it requires an embodiment of the truths of Jesus displayed in a real context, prepared to confront an aggressive world in chaos.

In light of such a context, it is with great appreciation and admiration that I read the writer's thoughts embodied in this precious book—one that not only presupposes but also assumes a very practical and contextual stance of the life and ministry of the incarnate Christ.

I love the way in which he presents its contents; he starts with "God's plan" and ends with "the plan" turned into a commandment. That is to say, the plan is God's project for the salvation for humans and the commandment is an imperative for the church to fulfill that missionary plan. However, in between he presents us with the activities of a holistic church. These two cannot be divorced. For example, the work of the Holy Spirit stimulates the life of one who is prepared through prayer and fasting for presenting the gospel in a concise, powerful, anointed, and incarnate way, as the fruit of his preparation.

He addresses the important issue of understanding the Scriptures as the foundation of knowledge for all servants who want to be true missionaries of the Kingdom. This knowledge draws us to the heart of God, and the Lord is revealed to those who seek him as he manifests his plan first hand. In simple words it could be said that the man or woman who does not know God can never be a holistic missionary.

Another important and key element: the church was created to fulfill God's amazing plan that we see at the start of this book. It definitely challenges us to embody all of Jesus' knowledge, truth, and experience into our lives so that we can "be" witnesses of Jesus and "be" missional.

I have known the writer for many years. He is my personal friend, and I have seen his passion and zeal for the Kingdom of God to be established in this decadent world. There is no one better to present this material, which has been the fruit of his own experience, but more than that, his way of life in word and in practice.

As such, I personally thank the Lord for his servants who are sensitive to the need and can share humbly, but incisively, truths to which the church needs to return with responsibility, objectivity, and a lot of passion.

PREFACE

I also recommend that this book to be considered as part of the coursework for missiology, evangelism, and leadership.

May the Lord bless and challenge each person who reads, studies, and shares this material. This is the prayer of the writer in his introduction: "In the process of writing this book, I asked God to make it an instrument of blessing to all the readers who are in faithful obedience and service in the fulfillment of the mission of the church."

—Rev. Leonel de Leon
Strategy Coordinator, North Central, Mesoamerica Region

INTRODUCTION

The idea to write a book on Jesus' principles for fulfilling the mission arose when I was appointed as Director of Multicultural Ministries for USA/Canada by the regional director, Dr. Bob Broadbooks, in May 2012. The privilege of my new assignment, along with being Director of Hispanic Ministries since 2002, would frame the responsibility of providing direction and strategic and logistical support to more than 16 ethnic and linguistic groups.

This new phase of ministerial life led me to seek, by prayer and fasting, God's direction on how to begin and perform my new assignment. I felt it would be very important to maintain contact with the leadership of the ethnic and linguistic groups and provide biblical inspiration for the fulfillment of the mission. Thus emerged the idea to design and establish a monthly electronic newsletter focused on the facilitators of the different ethnic groups and the members of their respective strategy committees. This newsletter would be a good means of presenting biblical reflections, news, events, statistics, prayer requests, etc.

Now that I had the vehicle—the e-newsletter—next would be to search for and provide the content for achieving the objective of the e-newsletter with the multicultural leadership. It was through this that I started to write a series of biblical reflections on "Jesus' Principles for Fulfilling the Mission." Every month I would look in the Gospels for a principle of how Jesus fulfilled his mission. I was fascinated and blessed by writing seven reflections, observing and following the principles that Jesus used in the fulfillment of the mission of the Kingdom of God.

Obviously, the principles I found were not entirely new to me. They were familiar subjects from the countless times that I have read the Gospels, the many times I watched the *Jesus* film, the books I have read, sermons I have heard, conferences I have attended, and conversations I have had with my colleagues. What was new for me was to write them down as a series of reflections on the principles Jesus applied in the fulfillment of his mission, to put them into a system.

In rereading the Gospels to find the principles Jesus used and how they were conveyed to his disciples for intentional training, this experience gave me a fresh perspective of the ministerial activity needed to follow the footsteps of the Master in the fulfillment of the mission, while at the same time leading me to think about the opportunity to expand these principles and put them in a simple book format, practical and in short chapters for reflection and application in pastoral ministry today.

In the process of writing this book, I asked God to make it an instrument of blessing to all the readers who are in faithful obedience and service in the fulfillment of the mission of the church.

CHAPTER 1

GOD'S PLAN

"

For God so loved the world that he gave his one and only Son, that whoever believes in him shall not perish but have eternal life. For God did not send his Son into the world to condemn the world, but to save the world through him. (John 3:16-17)

"

The creation story in Genesis tells about the harmony that existed between the Creator and his creation. After each act of creation, the writer exclaimed: "And God saw that it was good."

GENESIS 2:1-3 *"Thus the heavens and the earth were completed in all their vast array. By the seventh day God had finished the work he had been doing; so on the seventh day he*

> *rested from all his work. Then God blessed the seventh day and made it holy, because on it he rested from all the work of creating that he had done."*

God, the Creator, established an intimate and perfect relationship with Adam and Eve, who were made stewards of his creation. He also established a period of probation where Adam and Eve could exercise their free will to decide between good and evil. This period of probation was conditional on their obedience to the divine mandate.

> GENESIS 2:16-17 *"And the Lord God commanded the man, 'You are free to eat from any tree in the garden; but you must not eat from the tree of the knowledge of good and evil, for when you eat from it you will certainly die.'"*

If God was going to be glorified by the voluntary service of humans, then they must be put to the test—subjected to temptation—at the risk of the inevitable cost of the possibility of sin.[1] Unfortunately Adam and Eve chose to satisfy the desires of their eyes and ambitions and thus disobeyed that which was established by God. They gave in to temptation and Satan's deception that distorted the Word of God and made them fall in disobedience to God: *"Did God really say, 'You must not eat from any tree in the garden?'"*

Adam and Eve's disobedience produced serious consequences for the human race and for all of God's creation. The immediate consequences of their disobedience (their sin) was a break in the perfect harmony that existed between the Creator and his creation. The God of love and Creator came looking for Adam and Eve after they disobeyed him, and ever since, God has continuously been looking for ways to redeem the human race from the curse of sin and its consequences.

God, holy and full of love, had to hand down punishment for Adam and Eve for their disobedience. The holy nature of God cannot ignore the disobedience of sin. Yet, even in the act of punishment, God, who is just and merciful, punished with a plan of redemption:

> GENESIS 3:15 *"And I will put enmity between you and the woman, and between your offspring and hers; he will crush your head, and you will strike his heel."*

The phrase "you will strike his heel" refers to Satan's constant attempts to defeat Christ during his life on earth. "He will crush your head," announces Satan's defeat when Christ rose from the dead. A blow to the heel is not deadly, but one strike on the head certainly is. God was already revealing his plan to defeat Satan and offering salvation to the world through his Son, Jesus Christ.[2]

God was revealing the plan of redemption for his people throughout time. The prophets, spokesmen of God to the people of Israel and the nations, announced the coming of the Messiah, who would free them from sin and its consequences. The prophecies of the Messiah in the Old Testament writings are woven as a historical thread that point toward God's perfect plan of salvation, and would intersect the story of humanity in the person of the Messiah, Christ the Redeemer, the Anointed One of God.

> ISAIAH 43:1-4 *"But now, this is what the Lord says— he who created you, Jacob, he who formed you, Israel: 'Do not fear, for I have redeemed you; I have summoned you by name;*

> *you are mine. When you pass through the waters, I will be with you; and when you pass through the rivers, they will not sweep over you. When you walk through the fire, you will not be burned; the flames will not set you ablaze. For I am the Lord your God, the Holy One of Israel, your Savior; I give Egypt for your ransom, Cush and Seba in your stead. Since you are precious and honored in my sight, and because I love you, I will give people in exchange for you, nations in exchange for your life.'"*

The people of Israel lived with the expectation and hope of the future reign of the Messiah, and in their moments of great anguish and suffering, they were always looking for ways to sustain themselves in the promise of God's covenant that one day he would send his servant, the Messiah, to reign over and govern his people with justice. This historic promise of the Messiah encouraged them to trust and cope with the difficulties of their experiences in their history as the people of God.

In his perfect time, God fulfilled his promise to send the Messiah who was anticipated by the people of the father of the faith, Abraham and his descendants. God is faithful and fulfills all of his promises in his time. God would descend and become incarnate as part of the history of the human race in the person of Jesus, his Son, who would execute the perfect plan of redemption for all humankind.

> JOHN 1:14-16 *"The Word became flesh and made his dwelling among us. We have seen his glory, the glory of the one and only Son, who came from the Father, full of grace and truth. (John testified concerning him. He cried out, saying, 'This is the one I spoke about when I said, He who comes after me has surpassed me because he was be-*

GOD'S PLAN

fore me.') Out of his fullness we have all received grace in place of grace already given."

The apostle Peter gives witness to the living hope in Christ.

1 PETER 1:10-11 *"Concerning this salvation, the prophets, who spoke of the grace that was to come to you, searched intently and with the greatest care, trying to find out the time and circumstances to which the Spirit of Christ in them was pointing when he predicted the sufferings of the Messiah and the glories that would follow."*

He is truly God, but in the revelation of Christ, his human divinity is not separate of humanity; the divine and human natures never separated in him, nor did one neutralize the other. We see in Christ ... the fullness of the deity framed in the box of humanity; not being attributes of the divine in his limited infinity, rather the divine attributes taken form in the attributes of human nature."[3]

QUESTIONS FOR REFLECTION

1. How has this chapter on God's love and his plan of salvation for the redemption of the human race impacted you?
2. How have God's promises to his people in the person of Jesus Christ helped you?
3. What other biblical passages would you use for this chapter?
4. How have the prophecies about the Messiah inspired you?
5. On a scale of 1 to 10, with 10 being the highest score, answer this question: How do you currently feel about God's faithfulness and his promises for your life?

EXODUS 19:5-6 *"Now if you obey me fully and keep my covenant, then out of all nations you will be my treasured posses-*

sion. Although the whole earth is mine, you will be for me a kingdom of priests and a holy nation." These are the words you are to speak to the Israelites.

6. What should I do to trust in the promises of God?

Standing, Standing,
Standing on the promises of God my Savior;
Standing, standing,
I'm standing on the promises of God.

—*Sing to the Lord #687*

7. For further reflection on this chapter, if possible, take time to pray and study the scriptures you have found.

CHAPTER 2

THE HOLY SPIRIT

"

As soon as Jesus was baptized, he went up out of the water. At that moment heaven was opened, and he saw the Spirit of God descending like a dove and alighting on him. And a voice from heaven said, "This is my Son, whom I love; with him I am well pleased." (Matthew 3:16-17)

"

The Holy Spirit was sent to Jesus to publicly confirm that he was indeed the true Messiah from God's promise of salvation through his Son. The Triune God is present in the history of human redemption. The Holy Spirit would be in Jesus to guide him during his ministerial life. LUKE 4:1 *"Jesus, full of the Holy Spirit, left the Jordan and was led by the Spirit into the wilderness."* The Holy Spirit would be a faithful companion to Jesus in the fulfillment of the mission of the Kingdom of God. The Holy Spirit would give him strength to confront and resist the devil's temptations in the desert and during the rest of his ministry.

> Satan's temptations are focused on three things: (1) physical desires, (2) possessions and power, and (3) pride (you find a similar list in 1 John 2:15-16). But Jesus did not relent. Hebrews 4:15-16 says that Jesus was tempted ... but that he did not yield one time, and he did not sin. Jesus was able to resist all the temptations of Satan because he not only knew the Scriptures, but obeyed them (Ephesians 6:17).[1]

The period in the wilderness was necessary in preparing Jesus to start his ministry. First, he was intimately in communion with the Father through prayer and fasting. Second, when Satan came to tempt him he was able not only to defeat him by not sinning, but proving that it is possible not to succumb to the temptations and deceptions of the devil.

> LUKE 4:14-15 *"Jesus returned to Galilee in the power of the Spirit, and news about him spread through the whole countryside. He was teaching in their synagogues, and everyone praised him."*

It was necessary for Jesus to minister and teach under the direction of the Holy Spirit's power and anointing. Jesus was fulfilling the mission while at the same time showing by his example what is essential and indispensable for the Spirit's presence to effectively execute the mission of the Kingdom. Only by the help of the Holy Spirit could Jesus victoriously begin and culminate the mission of the Father.

THE HOLY SPIRIT

He was not the only one who worked through his humanity, it was also the temple of the Holy Spirit, whom God gave him without limits (John 3:34). Everything that belongs to the Son as representative of man was under the immediate direction of the Holy Spirit. The Holy Spirit guided and sustained him in each of the experiences of his earthly life, presiding over his entire ministry.[2]

Preparing his disciples for his departure, Jesus told them that the Holy Spirit would come upon them to accompany them in their daily living and comfort them in the most difficult moments of their lives.

> JOHN 16:7 *"But very truly I tell you, it is for your good that I am going away. Unless I go away, the Advocate will not come to you; but if I go, I will send him to you."*

Jesus knew how essential it would be for his disciples to have the presence of the Holy Spirit in their lives. The Holy Spirit would help the disciples be faithful and effective in fulfilling the mission. Time and again he insisted on the importance of the Holy Spirit's teaching for the lives of his followers.

> LUKE 24:49 *"I am going to send you what my Father has promised; but stay in the city until you have been clothed with power from on high."*

Through a parable, Jesus taught his disciples how they should seek the presence of the Holy Spirit in their lives. The Father wants to give them the Spirit, but it is up to them to apply this ardent desire to their hearts to receive it:

> LUKE 11:9-13 *"So I say to you: Ask and it will be given to you; seek and you will find; knock and the door will be opened to you. For everyone who asks receives; the one who seeks*

> *finds; and to the one who knocks, the door will be opened. Which of you fathers, if your son asks for a fish, will give him a snake instead? Or if he asks for an egg, will give him a scorpion? If you then, though you are evil, know how to give good gifts to your children, how much more will your Father in heaven give the Holy Spirit to those who ask him!"*

It was Jesus' desire that his disciples have what he had during his earthly ministry: the power and anointing of the Holy Spirit. It was the reason for these last words spoken to them before he ascended to the Father:

> ACTS 1:8-9 *"'But you will receive power when the Holy Spirit comes on you; and you will be my witnesses in Jerusalem, and in all Judea and Samaria, and to the ends of the earth.' After he said this, he was taken up before their very eyes, and a cloud hid him from their sight."*

The Day of Pentecost, the fulfillment of the promise of the coming of the Holy Spirit upon those who were obedient in awaiting his arrival, heralded a new era for the church in the Kingdom of God. The fulfillment of Jesus' promise, to send the Holy Spirit to his disciples, was accompanied by a series of supernatural events: a violent wind, tongues of fire, speaking in other languages, and hearing the good news in their own languages, culminating with the salvation of three thousand people, just as they are described in Acts.[3]

In the Old Testament God gave his Spirit to those whom he called to fulfill a specific mission among their people. The Holy Spirit was sent to a limited number of people providing them with supernatural power, as was the case of David:

THE HOLY SPIRIT

> 1 SAMUEL 16:13 *"So Samuel took the horn of oil and anointed him in the presence of his brothers, and from that day on the Spirit of the Lord came powerfully upon David."*

In the new dispensation of the church, the Holy Spirit is now available to everyone to guide, empower, and teach the church about everything related to the mission of God: JOHN 14:26 *"But the Advocate, the Holy Spirit, whom the Father will send in my name, will teach you all things and will remind you of everything I have said to you."* The church of Jesus Christ the Lord counts on the blessing of having the power of the Holy Spirit at its disposal. The book of Acts recounts the testimony of the power of the Holy Spirit over the church. In the difficult times of persecution, the church had the certainty that the Holy Spirit would strengthen and help them in fulfilling the mission:

> ACTS 4:29-31 *"'Now, Lord, consider their threats and enable your servants to speak your word with great boldness. Stretch out your hand to heal and perform signs and wonders through the name of your holy servant Jesus.' After they prayed, the place where they were meeting was shaken. And they were all filled with the Holy Spirit and spoke the word of God boldly."*

The early church was guided and accompanied by the Spirit to advance the mission of the Kingdom, and its members were filled with the Spirit's power. The first martyr recorded in the history of the church was Stephen, *"a man full of God's grace and power, [who] performed great wonders and signs among the people."* The Holy Spirit helped the church fulfill its purpose of being witnesses wherever they went as well as in threatening circumstances they experienced, as in the case of Philip when he fled from the persecution that erupted in Jerusalem:

> Acts 8:5-8 *"Philip went down to a city in Samaria and proclaimed the Messiah there. When the crowds heard Philip and saw the signs he performed, they all paid close attention to what he said. For with shrieks, impure spirits came out of many, and many who were paralyzed or lame were healed. So there was great joy in that city."*

The apostle Paul was ministering in the power of the Spirit and stated that his preaching did not depend on his human knowledge but in the power of God.

> 1 Corinthians 2:4-5 *"My message and my preaching were not with wise and persuasive words, but with a demonstration of the Spirit's power, so that your faith might not rest on human wisdom, but on God's power."*

The apostle Paul reminds the church in Thessalonica how they were told about this good news:

> 1 Thessalonians 1:5 *"because our gospel came to you not simply with words but also with power, with the Holy Spirit and deep conviction. You know how we lived among you for your sake."*

The Holy Spirit is the indispensable source of power of the church to effectively and faithfully fulfill the mission of the Kingdom. "The Holy Spirit convicts us, cleans us, fills us and gives power as the grace of God transforms us day after day into a community of love, spiritual discipline, purity, ethics, moral rectitude, compassion and justice."[3] The church absolutely has to rely on the power of the Holy Spirit to confront the oppositions of darkness and advance the Kingdom of God, just as Jesus and the early church did. The biographies of the great servants of God that made a huge impact on the establishment and progression of the mission of the church testify to an extraordinary experience with the Holy Spirit.

James Hervey, one of John Wesley's ministry colleagues, uses these words to narrate the difference made by the Holy Spirit in Wesley's ministry:

> Although his preaching had been as the firing of an arrow, totally dependent on the strength and speed of his arm in order to draw the arrow back, it was now like shooting a rifle bullet in that the full force depended on the power that only needed a finger to pull the trigger.[4]

Phineas E. Bresee, founder of the Church of the Nazarene, told the writer of his biography, Carl Bangs, about an extraordinary experience with the Holy Spirit that happened two years after his pastorate at the Church of Fort, California:

> In spite of the success I had, I was continuously and sincerely praying, asking God to give me an experience that would satisfy my needs. One evening I sat in the living room of my house and I began to pray and, after a while, a ball of fire like a meteorite came toward me, and I heard a voice tell me, "drink, drink," and it instantly covered my face and lips. I tried to obey the voice and sipped a little and a sensation like that of a fire was maintained in me for several days. That transformed my heart and was a blessing to my life and was a glorious anointing which I had never experienced before. I felt that the need of satisfaction that I was looking for in my life had been met. That brought a new spiritual element and power into my life. After this experience I saw to it that more people were converted.[5]

These two great heroes of faith made a huge impact in the progress of the mission of the Kingdom of God in their times and transcended the borders where they carried out their ministries. Today, those who proclaim a theological and doctrinal heritage from these two servants of God seek an experience with the Holy Spirit in the fulfillment of the mission.

> Oh, my fellow Christian colleagues! We need to be soaked with a new shedding of the Spirit on us; we need the power of God to fall on us again and again, to come into us, to fill us and saturate us until we can truly say about our lives, "not I, but Christ" and in our ministries "not I, but the Spirit of God."[6]

QUESTIONS FOR REFLECTION

1. How has this chapter about Jesus' life and ministry upon receiving the Holy Spirit to accompany him with power and anointing impacted you in the fulfillment of the mission?
2. How has Jesus' promise of the Holy Spirit to his disciples helped you?
3. What other biblical passages would you use for this chapter?
4. How have the lives of God's servants filled with the Holy Spirit inspired you in fulfilling the mission?
5. On a scale of 1 to 10, with 10 being the highest score, answer this question: How do you currently feel about the Holy Spirit's power and anointing in your life in the fulfillment of the mission?

> ZECHARIAH 4:6 *"So he said to me, 'This is the word of the Lord to Zerubbabel: "Not by might nor by power, but by my Spirit," says the Lord Almighty.'"*

6. What should I do to keep the anointing and power of the Holy Spirit fresh in my life for fulfilling the mission?

O I never shall forget how the fire fell,
How the fire fell,
O I never shall forget how the fire fell,
When the Lord sanctified me.

—*Sing to the Lord #506*

7. For further reflection on this chapter, if possible, take time to pray and study the scriptures you have found.

CHAPTER 3

THE SCRIPTURES

"

You study the Scriptures diligently because you think that in them you have eternal life. These are the very Scriptures that testify about me. (John 5:39)

"

Jesus had a full understanding of the sacred Scriptures, and he continuously referenced them in the fulfillment of the mission. At an early age, he had conversations with doctors of the law, who were the scholars and interpreters of the sacred books for the people of God.

LUKE 2:46 *"After three days they found him in the temple courts, sitting among the teachers, listening to them and asking them questions."*

FULFILLING THE MISSION

In his confrontation with Satan in the desert, Jesus emerged victorious against the deception and snares of the devil, quoting the Holy Scriptures: ^{MATTHEW 4:4} *"Jesus answered, 'It is written: Man shall not live on bread alone, but on every word that comes from the mouth of God.'"* Each time Satan offered something to tempt him, Jesus answered with certainty: *"It is also written: 'Do not put the Lord your God to the test.'"*

Jesus visited the synagogues and affirmed the teachings of the Scriptures.

> The synagogues were very important in the religious life of the Jews. During the exile when the Jews could not enjoy the temple, the synagogues were established as places for worship on Saturdays and as schools for children during the week.[1]

Luke recorded the story of when Jesus visited the synagogue and was given the book of the prophet Isaiah to read. Here, a reference to the announcement of the coming of the Messiah is found (Isaiah 61:1-2). Upon reading the Scriptures Jesus concluded by saying: "Today this scripture is fulfilled in your hearing."

The religious Sadducees, who did not believe in the resurrection, held their own interpretation about life after death. The Sadducees came to Jesus with a question, asking if there is a resurrection of the dead or not, and referenced the law of Moses in order to present their opposition to belief in the resurrection. But Jesus corrected their wrong interpretation by using Scriptures:

> ^{MARK 12:24-27} *"Are you not in error because you do not know the Scriptures or the power of God? When the dead rise, they will neither marry nor be given in marriage; they will be*

THE SCRIPTURES

> *like the angels in heaven. Now about the dead rising— have you not read in the Book of Moses, in the account of the burning bush, how God said to him, 'I am the God of Abraham, the God of Isaac, and the God of Jacob'? He is not the God of the dead, but of the living. You are badly mistaken!"*

Jesus taught his disciples the fundamentals of the Scriptures and, after his resurrection, appeared to two of them to confirm.

> LUKE 24:27 *"And beginning with Moses and all the Prophets, he explained to them what was said in all the Scriptures concerning himself."*

The apostles used the Scriptures to bear witness to God's plan in the person of his Son, Jesus Christ. On the day of Pentecost, the apostle Peter made reference to the Scriptures, explaining the phenomenon of the coming of the Holy Spirit:

> ACTS 2:16-18 *"This is what was spoken by the prophet Joel: 'In the last days, God says, I will pour out my Spirit on all people. Your sons and daughters will prophesy, your young men will see visions, your old men will dream dreams. Even on my servants, both men and women, I will pour out my Spirit in those days, and they will prophesy.'"*

Philip, the deacon, used Scripture in order to evangelize the eunuch of Ethiopia.

> ACTS 8:35 *"Then Philip began with that very passage of Scripture and told him the good news about Jesus."*

When the apostle Paul came to the city of Berea, he taught them about Jesus Christ by means of the Scriptures:

> ACTS 17:11-12 *"Now the Berean Jews were of more noble character than those in Thessalonica, for they received the message*

> with great eagerness and examined the Scriptures every day to see if what Paul said was true. As a result, many of them believed, as did also a number of prominent Greek women and many Greek men."

The source of the doctrinal teachings of the early church for God's plan of salvation in the person of Jesus Christ was founded in the sacred books of the Scriptures:

> 1 CORINTHIANS 15:3-4 *"For what I received I passed on to you as of first importance: that Christ died for our sins according to the Scriptures, that he was buried, that he was raised on the third day according to the Scriptures."*

Throughout history, the church has tried to keep the cardinal doctrines based on the source of the revelations of the holy Scriptures. The articles of faith of the *Manual* of the Church of the Nazarene state the following:

> We believe in the plenary inspiration of the Holy Scriptures, by which we understand the 66 books of the Old and New Testaments, given by divine inspiration, inerrantly revealing the will of God concerning us in all things necessary to our salvation, so that whatever is not contained therein is not to be enjoined as an article of faith.[2]

The men and women that God has used to impact his world, those who have lived under the conviction of the divine revelation of the Scriptures, such as Martin Luther and John Wesley and others have stated that their lives and teachings are based on "Scripture alone." John Wesley said, "I am a man of one book."

> Knowing and obeying the Word of God serves as an effective weapon against temptation, the only offensive piece of the "armor" of God (Ephesians 6:17). Jesus used Scripture to deal with

THE SCRIPTURES

Satan's attacks and you can, too. But in order to be effective, you must have faith in the promises of God because Satan also knows the Scriptures and is an expert in twisting them to suit his purpose. Obeying the Scriptures is much more important than knowing a simple verse to quote. Read them daily and apply them to your life. This way your "sword" will always be sharp.[3]

QUESTIONS FOR REFLECTION

1. How has this chapter impacted you about how Jesus used the Scriptures in the fulfillment of the mission?
2. How have Jesus' teachings to his disciples about the Scriptures helped you?
3. What other biblical passages would you use for this chapter?
4. How have the apostles use of the Scriptures in the fulfillment of the mission inspired you?
5. On a scale of 1 to 10, with 10 being the highest score, answer this question: How much do you use the Scriptures in the fulfillment of the mission?

   JOSHUA 1:8 *"Keep this Book of the Law always on your lips; meditate on it day and night, so that you may be careful to do everything written in it. Then you will be prosperous and successful."*

6. How can I keep up with reading the Scriptures in my devotional life?

Holy Bible, Book divine,
Precious treasure, thou art mine:
Mine to tell me whence I came;
Mine to teach me what I am.
   —*"Holy Bible, Book Divine," cyberhymnal.org, #324*

7. For further reflection on this chapter, if possible, take time to pray and study the scriptures you have found.

CHAPTER 4

THE INTIMATE RELATIONSHIP WITH THE FATHER

"

The one who sent me is with me; he has not left me alone, for I always do what pleases him. Even as he spoke, many believed in him. (John 8:29-30)

"

Throughout his ministry, Jesus lived in total dependence and relationship with the Father. His relationship was an example of someone completely submitted to the authority of God, who had sent him to fulfill the mission of the Kingdom. This dependence on the Father showed that it was not his own will but his Father's will.

From an early age, Jesus established that he came to do the will of the Father. On one occasion in which Jesus was with his earthly parents for the Passover celebration, he sought the opportunity to talk with the scholars of the law. He was so interested that apparently he lost track of time to return to Nazareth with his parents.

> Those who attended these festivities often traveled in caravans to guard against assaults along the roads of Palestine. It was the custom for women and children to travel at the front of the motorcade and the men would be in the rear. At twelve years old, a boy could participate in either of the two groups and Joseph and Mary each thought that Jesus was in the other group. But when the caravan was leaving Jerusalem, Jesus was captivated by the discussion with the religious leaders.[1]

After having walked for a day, Joseph and Mary noticed that the boy Jesus was not in the group of travelers returning to their city. Obviously they got worried and decided to return to Jerusalem where they found him.

> LUKE 2:48-49 *"His mother said to him, 'Son, why have you treated us like this? Your father and I have been anxiously searching for you.'*
>
> *'Why were you searching for me?' he asked. 'Didn't you know I had to be in my Father's house?'"*

Jesus identified fully with the Father and was able to say that he was his manifestation.

THE INTIMATE RELATIONSHIP WITH THE FATHER

> JOHN 14:7 *"If you really know me, you will know my Father as well. From now on, you do know him and have seen him."*

Only the child who has the security of an intimate relationship with his or her father is able to announce with confidence, "If you really know me, you will know my Father as well." Jesus had the certainty that everything he did and taught about the mission of the Kingdom was in obedience to the Father. He told Philip, one of his disciples:

> JOHN 14:10-11 *"Don't you believe that I am in the Father, and that the Father is in me? The words I say to you I do not speak on my own authority. Rather, it is the Father, living in me, who is doing his work. Believe me when I say that I am in the Father and the Father is in me; or at least believe on the evidence of the works themselves."*

As the son, he voluntarily submits to the authority of the Father and declares: "The Father is greater than I" (John 14:28). Thus, there is perfect harmony in the Deity. Joyfully, the Father takes the place at the head and the Son responds with obedience.[2]

Jesus' message of the good news of the Kingdom was to bring to light the merciful and loving Father, one who wants the best for his children and the human race. The miracles that Jesus did of physical healing, casting out demons, forgiving of sins and others were done so that they would get to know the Father's will and believe in him. Only a child who has a confident relationship with his or her father dares to invite friends to come to live with his or her house. This is what did. He invites his disciples to come to live with him in his Father's house:

> JOHN 14:1-3 *"Do not let your hearts be troubled. You believe in God; believe also in me. My Father's house has many rooms; if that were not so, would I have told you that I am going there to prepare a place for you? And if I go and prepare a place for you, I will come back and take you to be with me that you also may be where I am."*

Jesus walked intimately with the Father until the last moments of his life before going to the cross for the redemption of humanity. Jesus knew where to go in the moments of agony and pain; he was going to the Father.

> MARK 14:35-36 *"Going a little farther, he fell to the ground and prayed that if possible the hour might pass from him. 'Abba, Father,' he said, 'everything is possible for you. Take this cup from me. Yet not what I will, but what you will.'"*

In his last words on the cross Jesus gave up his spirit and told his Father that he had completed the mission for which he had been sent: *"'It is finished.' With that, he bowed his head and gave up his spirit."*

Jesus wanted his disciples to have confidence in him and in the Father, just as he did.

> JOHN 14:13-14 *"And I will do whatever you ask in my name, so that the Father may be glorified in the Son. You may ask me for anything in my name, and I will do it."*

The Lord's disciples lived in total dependence on the Father just as Jesus had taught by example. The apostle John wrote to the church in 1 John 1:3: *"We proclaim to you what we have seen and heard, so that you also may have fellowship with us. And our fellowship is with the Father and with his Son, Jesus Christ."*

THE INTIMATE RELATIONSHIP WITH THE FATHER

The apostle Paul makes the following statement:

> 1 CORINTHIANS 8:5-6 *"For even if there are so-called gods, whether in heaven or on earth (as indeed there are many 'gods' and many 'lords'), yet for us there is but one God, the Father, from whom all things came and for whom we live; and there is but one Lord, Jesus Christ, through whom all things came and through whom we live."*

In the book of James we find the following reference:

> JAMES 1:17-18 *"Every good and perfect gift is from above, coming down from the Father of the heavenly lights, who does not change like shifting shadows. He chose to give us birth through the word of truth, that we might be a kind of firstfruits of all he created."*

Jesus' teachings about the Father penetrated the life of the early church. God's servants learn to live in total dependence through an intimate relationship with the Father. They do not rely on their own abilities and knowledge but rather in total submission to him.

> God reveals himself as a loving Father, close to his children, and sensitive to their needs, therefore he teaches, loves, helps and heals them. Growth is not something that God leaves to chance; the Lord consciously *nourishes* his children. God's feeling toward his children is represented in the meaning behind the name of Hosea: "liberator" or "helper." The Hebrew root word *yasha* indicates that freedom or help is provided by grace and is free, and in turn provides a safe haven for every child of God.[3]

QUESTIONS FOR REFLECTION

1. How has this chapter about the intimate relationship Jesus had with the Father in the fulfillment of the mission impacted you?
2. How have Jesus' teachings to his disciples about the Scriptures helped you?
3. What other biblical passages would you use for this chapter?
4. How have the teachings of the apostles about the Father inspired you?
5. On a scale of 1 to 10, with 10 being the highest score, answer this question: How much do you depend on the Father in the fulfillment of the mission?

   ISAIAH 63:16 *"But you are our Father, though Abraham does not know us or Israel acknowledge us; you, Lord, are our Father, our Redeemer from of old is your name."*

6. How can I maintain a trustworthy and intimate relationship with the Father?

Come Thou Almighty King
Help us Thy name to sing.
Help us to praise.
Father all glorious
O'er all victorious
Come, and reign over us
Ancient of Days.

—*Sing to the Lord #3*

7. For further reflection on this chapter, if possible, take time to pray and study the scriptures you have found.

CHAPTER 5

PRAYER AND FASTING

> *Very early in the morning, while it was still dark, Jesus got up, left the house and went off to a solitary place, where he prayed. Simon and his companions went to look for him, and when they found him, they exclaimed: "Everyone is looking for you!" Jesus replied, "Let us go somewhere else—to the nearby villages—so I can preach there also. That is why I have come." So he traveled throughout Galilee, preaching in their synagogues and driving out demons.* (Mark 1:35-39)

Jesus practiced a disciplined life of prayer and fasting in the fulfillment of the mission. Prayer was the manner by which Jesus was in constant communion with the Father. Prayer was essential in his life and ministry. The Gospels describe Jesus as being in prayer all the time. The most important thing for him was to start his day in prayer. He would look for a deserted place so that he could concentrate and avoid distractions or those who would interrupt his conversation with the Father.

Jesus preached the message of the Kingdom with authority and spent special time alone with the Father to meditate and prepare his heart for the word that he would convey to his listeners. In confrontation with demons, Jesus was strengthened in power through prayer and fasting and was able to cast them away and release those who were oppressed by these evil spirits. Jesus practiced prayer as a spiritual discipline which gave him the power and authority of the Father and of the Holy Spirit to heal the sick. The writer of the Gospel of Luke presents Jesus' devotional life in the fulfillment of the mission:

> LUKE 5:15-16 *"Yet the news about him spread all the more, so that crowds of people came to hear him and to be healed of their sicknesses. But Jesus often withdrew to lonely places and prayed."*

Jesus not only disciplined himself to pray in the mornings, but also after a long day of ministry. On one occasion he had spent long hours teaching the crowds and was undoubtedly very tired, but he knew how to receive renewed strength by spending time in prayer and giving thanks to the Father.

> MATTHEW 15:23 *"After he had dismissed them, he went up on a mountainside by himself to pray. Later that night, he was there alone."*

Jesus also prayed for the Father's blessing in public as seen in the miracle of multiplying a few loaves and fish to feed the huge crowd that had gathered to hear him. After a long day Jesus wanted to finish his teachings by meeting the basic need of food.

> MATTHEW 14:19 *"And he directed the people to sit down on the grass. Taking the five loaves and the two fish and looking up to heaven, he gave thanks and broke the loaves. Then he gave them to the disciples, and the disciples gave them to the people."*

On several occasions Jesus invited his disciples to accompany him to pray, and by doing so, he taught his disciples what was essential for prayer, not only individually but collectively. Jesus took advantage of every opportunity to train his disciples who would go on to guide his church:

> LUKE 9:18-20 *"Once when Jesus was praying in private and his disciples were with him, he asked them, 'Who do the crowds say I am?' They replied, 'Some say John the Baptist; others say Elijah; and still others, that one of the prophets of long ago has come back to life.'*
>
> *'But what about you?' he asked. 'Who do you say I am?'*
>
> *Peter answered, 'God's Messiah.'"*

Jesus' exemplary life of prayer impacted his disciples, who sought a disciplined life of prayer just like their Master. Upon seeing Jesus' dedication and consistency, they wanted to be like him, therefore asking him to teach them to pray. On that occasion Jesus introduced the "Our Father" prayer.

> LUKE 11:1-4 *"One day Jesus was praying in a certain place. When he finished, one of his disciples said to him, 'Lord, teach us to pray, just as John taught his disciples.'*
>
> *He said to them, 'When you pray, say: "Father, hallowed be your name, your Kingdom come. Give us each day our*

> *daily bread. Forgive us our sins, for we also forgive everyone who sins against us. And lead us not into temptation."'"*

Rabbis would use prayer to prepare and cultivate their disciples' spiritual lives; Jesus gave his disciples the model for prayer to draw them to the Father.

> This prayer can serve as a model for our prayers. We should praise God, pray for his work in the world, pray for our daily needs, and pray for his help in our daily conflicts. The phrase "Our Father who is in heaven" indicates that God is not only majestic and holy, but also personal and loving. The first line of this model prayer is a declaration of praise and dedication to honor the holy name of God.[1]

The disciples learned the lesson of the model prayer very well, starting first by recognizing the greatness of the holy and almighty God. Even in the most critical times when they found themselves under threats and persecution, the church did not forget to start with prayer and praise to the God of all creation.

> Acts 4:24 *"When they heard this, they raised their voices together in prayer to God. 'Sovereign Lord,' they said, 'you made the heavens and the earth and the sea, and everything in them.'"*

On another occasion an anxious parent brought his son to the disciples to be healed. Jesus was not around at that time and the disciples tried to heal him, but they were unable to do so in that situation. When Jesus came, the father of the young man said to him:

> Matthew 17:15-21 *"Lord, have mercy on my son," he said. "He has seizures and is suffering greatly. He often falls into the*

> *fire or into the water. I brought him to your disciples, but they could not heal him."*
>
> *"You unbelieving and perverse generation," Jesus replied, "how long shall I stay with you? How long shall I put up with you? Bring the boy here to me." Jesus rebuked the demon, and it came out of the boy, and he was healed at that moment.*
>
> *Then the disciples came to Jesus in private and asked, "Why couldn't we drive it out?"*
>
> *He replied, "Because you have so little faith. Truly I tell you, if you have faith as small as a mustard seed, you can say to this mountain, 'Move from here to there,' and it will move. Nothing will be impossible for you."*

Jesus used that opportunity to emphasize to his disciples the essence of prayer and fasting in their lives so that they too would be able to confront difficult situations like this boy possessed by a demon. The apostles needed to put all the teachings of the Master into practice and in their guidance of the early church. As the church grew, they encountered challenges, such as complaints and grumblings about the lack of attention to the widows and orphans. The case was presented to the apostles in order to find a solution to this problem in the new community of faith.

After consulting, the apostles opted to delegate the responsibility of food distribution for the widows to a group of men filled with the Holy Spirit so that they could be free to devote themselves to the more important task of guiding the church: ACTS 6:4 *"[We] will give our attention to prayer and the ministry of the word"*. The disciples had learned from the Master that in order to fulfill the mission of the Kingdom, a life consecrated and devoted to prayer and to proclaiming the good news of the Kingdom was required.

The apostle Paul was a man of prayer and fasting, who urged the church to live this spiritual discipline.

> PHILIPPIANS 4:6 *"Do not be anxious about anything, but in every situation, by prayer and petition, with thanksgiving, present your requests to God."*
>
> 2 CORINTHIANS 6:4-5 *"Rather, as servants of God we commend ourselves in every way: in great endurance; in troubles, hardships and distresses; in beatings, imprisonments and riots; in hard work, sleepless nights and hunger."*

God has used men and women in a very special way to birth great works of revival. One of the characteristics of their lives has been the spiritual discipline of prayer and fasting. They ministered under and depended on a life of prayer and fasting as they fulfilled the mission. These men and women have left their mark on the church through the impact they had on the people of their time. Men of God such as Charles G. Finney:

> After having been ordained in 1824, he held his first regular meetings in a place in New York City where he preached for several weeks without results. Finney spent the next day in fasting and prayer and, that night, an unusual sense of anointing and power came over him. ... Throughout the night people who were wanting prayer searched for him so that he could go and pray with them, even hardened atheists repented and were saved.[2]

Another was a Scottish man named Duncan Campbell, who was used powerfully by God to start a revival in the Hebrides Islands which began December 1949 and continued in subsequent years:

Duncan faced stiff opposition when he began the ministry in one of the Scottish islands. He walked the pathways at night praying and asking God for help. Three young people received a burden to pray, and they prayed all night in their homes while Duncan did the same in a stable. The following afternoon the power of God fell on their meetings. The people were so overcome by the conviction of the Holy Spirit, they were begging and pleading for mercy.[3]

John Wesley left a legacy with his devotional life of prayer and fasting. Wesley not only practiced the discipline of prayer and fasting, he also wanted all of his ministers to do the same, to the degree that it was one of the questions he would ask of his ministers: "Have you been fasting and praying for a few days? Go to the throne of grace and persevere there, then mercy will descend."[4]

A godly minister in the Church of Scotland, Robert Murray McCheyne, said: "It is better, in general, to spend an hour alone with God before committing to anything else. I should spend the better hours of the day in communion with God."[5]

QUESTIONS FOR REFLECTION

1. How has this chapter about Jesus' life of prayer and fasting in the fulfillment of the mission impacted you?
2. How have Jesus' teachings about prayer and fasting helped you?
3. What other biblical passages would you use for this chapter?
4. How have the teachings and practices of the apostles and the servants of God about prayer and fasting impacted you?

5. On a scale of 1 to 10, with 10 being the highest score, answer this question: How much do you practice the spiritual discipline of prayer and fasting?

   NEHEMIAH 1:4-6 *"When I heard these things, I sat down and wept. For some days I mourned and fasted and prayed before the God of heaven. Then I said: 'Lord, the God of heaven, the great and awesome God, who keeps his covenant of love with those who love him and keep his commandments, let your ear be attentive and your eyes open to hear the prayer your servant is praying before you.'"*

6. Ask yourself: How can I have a life of prayer and fasting?

   Prayer is the breath of the soul's deep life,
   Pray, pray, pray;
   Prayer is the shield in the midst of strife,
   Pray, pray, pray;
   Pray when about you the clouds hang low,
   Pray when you know not which way to go;
   God's holy will you may surely know,
   If you pray, pray, pray.

   —*Hymn, "Holy," hymnary.org*

7. For further reflection on this chapter, if possible, take time to pray and study the scriptures you have found.

CHAPTER 6

THE ELECTION OF THE APOSTLES

"

One of those days Jesus went out to a mountainside to pray, and spent the night praying to God. When morning came, he called his disciples to him and chose twelve of them, whom he also designated apostles. (Luke 6:12-13)

"

Jesus called and chose a group of men to accompany him in accomplishing the mission. These men came from different professional and socio-economic backgrounds. The disciples were not the best equipped or most qualified, but Jesus saw great potential for the mission of the Kingdom in them.

FULFILLING THE MISSION

The Gospels describe the disciples' assorted personalities and professions. They were not the religious elite with academic credentials or preparation, nor were they economically privileged. Several of the disciples were rustic sea men dedicated to fishing as a profession, who were accustomed to the challenges of fishing in the sea of Galilee at night.

> MATTHEW 4:18-22 *"As Jesus was walking beside the Sea of Galilee, he saw two brothers, Simon called Peter and his brother Andrew. They were casting a net into the lake, for they were fishermen. 'Come, follow me,' Jesus said, 'and I will send you out to fish for people.' At once they left their nets and followed him.*
>
> *Going on from there, he saw two other brothers, James son of Zebedee and his brother John. They were in a boat with their father Zebedee, preparing their nets. Jesus called them, and immediately they left the boat and their father and followed him."*

One of the disciples came from a profession that did not have good reputation among the Jews: LUKE 5:27-28 *"After this, Jesus went out and saw a tax collector by the name of Levi sitting at his tax booth. 'Follow me,' Jesus said to him, and Levi got up, left everything and followed him."* This man served the interests of the Roman government and demanded taxes from the Jewish citizens to sustain the pleasures and idolatry of the empire.

Jesus would go on to spend the next three years of his ministry preparing this group of men to help him fulfill and accomplish the mission. Although they were not the most qualified, Jesus knew that by investing time and energy in them, they would become the messengers of the good news of the Kingdom.

THE ELECTION OF THE APOSTLES

> LUKE 9:1-6 *"When Jesus had called the Twelve together, he gave them power and authority to drive out all demons and to cure diseases, and he sent them out to proclaim the Kingdom of God and to heal the sick. He told them: 'Take nothing for the journey—no staff, no bag, no bread, no money, no extra shirt. Whatever house you enter, stay there until you leave that town. If people do not welcome you, leave their town and shake the dust off your feet as a testimony against them.' So they set out and went from village to village, proclaiming the good news and healing people everywhere."*

Because of his humanity, Jesus could not be in different places at the same time and was aware that his ministry would be for a short period of time. The best strategy for Jesus to establish and advance his mission with greater effectiveness was to cultivate his disciples in the fulfillment of the mission.

Jesus sent his disciples with his power and authority to do the same as he did: to preach the good news of the Kingdom, cast out demons and heal the sick. Fishermen, tax collectors, activists like Judas the Zealot, and the other disciples would be the voice, feet, and hands of the Master. He was multiplying himself in them. They would become leaders taking the teachings and truths of the Kingdom to different cities and neighborhoods in Israel. Jesus chose these men—who were not academics and had no religious credentials—so that the glory would not be for them but for himself, the Master, who sent them. The disciples effectively fulfilled this mission.

These ordinary men from Galilee would carry forward the mission of the church of Jesus Christ. They would be recognized even by the rulers and the religious authorities of Jerusalem.

FULFILLING THE MISSION

> Acts 4:13 *"When they saw the courage of Peter and John and realized that they were unschooled, ordinary men, they were astonished and they took note that these men had been with Jesus."*

They had spent time with Jesus and it was clear to everyone that the Master had been reproduced in his disciples. The disciples came to be a force no religious or political structure could stop in the advancement of the mission of the Kingdom. Jesus had trained them for the mission. They were guided by the power of the Holy Spirit and were cementing the foundational teachings of the church.

> Acts 2:41-42 *"Those who accepted his message were baptized, and about three thousand were added to their number that day. They devoted themselves to the apostles' teaching and to fellowship, to the breaking of bread and to prayer."*

Before Jesus called the apostles, they had little or no administrative or theological preparation; now they were leading and directing the movement of the new Christian faith and attending to the essential affairs of the church. The Master had shaped them with the values and principles of the Kingdom to carry forward the mission of the church.

There was a major argument in the church over how the teachings would apply to converts to this new Christianity, particularly those who had no background in the Jewish religion. With the Spirit's wisdom and help, the apostles deliberated and reached a consensus on how to adapt the teachings of Judaism to the new faith in Jesus Christ. They sent their resolution to the churches so that they could be structured using the same practices and would not impose additional elements of Judaism.

THE ELECTION OF THE APOSTLES

> ACTS 15:22-23 *"Then the apostles and elders, with the whole church, decided to choose some of their own men and send them to Antioch with Paul and Barnabas. They chose Judas (called Barsabbas) and Silas, men who were leaders among the believers. With them they sent the following letter."*

This new Christian faith would become the most influential religious movement in the whole of human history. The disciples, ordinary men, succeeded in their teachings and did extraordinary things under the authority of the Master, Jesus Christ, and in the power of his Spirit.

The apostle Paul applied the same principle of discipleship. He knew that it was the most effective strategy the Master used to train his disciples in the establishment and advancement of the Kingdom of God. Paul selected a group of men and women in whom to invest and, in this way, continue the expansion of the mission of the church. Specifically, he advised Timothy to be devoted to the training of other people for the fulfillment of the mission of the church.

> 2 TIMOTHY 2:1-2 *"You then, my son, be strong in the grace that is in Christ Jesus. And the things you have heard me say in the presence of many witnesses entrust to reliable people who will also be qualified to teach others."*

Throughout Christian history there have been movements guided by men and women that impacted their communities and the world, using the disciples' principles for training and multiplication. John Wesley realized the importance of Jesus' principle of discipleship of investing time for training. He, too, devoted time to train a group of people who would help to advance a new movement that would come to be known as the Wesleyan Methodist Church.

The Master's Plan is being used today as a biblical strategy for evangelism and discipleship. This program follows the steps that Jesus, Paul, Timothy, Wesley, and others have used for training leaders in the fulfillment of the mission. "The purpose of *The Master's Plan* is to win the community by means of the gospel of Jesus Christ, consolidating new believers so that they may remain faithful and obedient to the Lord and being trained to be sent as Christlike disciples of Jesus."[1]

> Discipleship is the trip of a lifetime into obedience to Christ that transforms the values and behavior of a person, which, as a result, produces ministry in the home, the church, and the world. It is a process for teaching new citizens of the Kingdom of God how to love, trust and obey God, and by which they are taught to win and train others to do the same.[2]

QUESTIONS FOR REFLECTION

1. How has this chapter about how Jesus chose the disciples to help him fulfill the mission impacted you?
2. How have Jesus' teachings about discipleship helped you?
3. What other biblical passages would you use for this chapter?
4. How have the teachings and practices about discipleship from the apostles and other servants of God impacted you?
5. On a scale of 1 to 10, with 10 being the highest score, answer this question: Do you practice the principle of discipleship with your leaders?

1 KINGS 19:19-20A *"So Elijah went from there and found Elisha son of Shaphat. He was plowing with twelve yoke of oxen,*

THE ELECTION OF THE APOSTLES

and he himself was driving the twelfth pair. Elijah went up to him and threw his cloak around him. Elisha then left his oxen and ran after Elijah."

6. What should I do to practice the ministry of making Christlike disciples?

O to be like Thee! O to be like Thee,
Blessed Redeemer, pure as Thou art!
Come in Thy sweetness; come in Thy fullness.
Stamp Thine own image deep on my heart.
—*Sing to the Lord, #490*

7. For further reflection on this chapter, if possible, take time to pray and study the scriptures you have found.

CHAPTER 7

PREACHING AND THE MOVEMENT OF THE KINGDOM OF GOD

"

Jesus replied, "Go back and report to John what you hear and see: The blind receive sight, the lame walk, those who have leprosy are cleansed, the deaf hear, the dead are raised, and the good news is proclaimed to the poor." (Matthew 11:4-5)

"

Jesus came to preach and teach the eternal truths of the Kingdom of God. The crowds followed him in order to listen to these new teachings of God's revelation through his Son. They were hungry and eager to listen to Jesus. The prophet from

Galilee talked to them with authority *from* heaven *about* heaven. The announcement of the preaching of the Kingdom was introduced by John the Baptist in anticipation of the Messiah's ministry.

> John came preaching repentance because the Kingdom of God was nearing (Matthew 3:2). Being an Israelite would not ensure entry into the Kingdom. In addition, the appropriate works should accompany repentance (Luke 3:8). Judgment was near, the ax was already set to the root of the trees (Luke 3:9). Despite the apparent similarity between this message and the one that Jesus would present a little later, John still imagined a political and worldly Kingdom. When he saw no evidence of that Kingdom, John sent messengers to ask Jesus about this (Matthew 11:2). Jesus, in effect, replied that the presence of the Kingdom of God was verified in healing the sick, the resurrection of the dead and in the preaching of the gospel to the poor (Matthew 11:4). The character of the Kingdom that Jesus brought was not political, literal, or earthly but was evidenced in works that pointed toward a complete restoration.[1]

The teachings of Jesus about the Kingdom of God were very different from those of the religious leaders of his time. They also differed from the popular and political teachings about the restoration of the Davidic Kingdom with a demonstration of political liberation free from all taxation and foreign powers.

> Between the two testaments (old and new) emerged a marked messianism which proclaimed the restoration of Israel's reign. This renewed hope took many forms, but the most common was the one from the pseudepigraphic book *Song of Songs:* the son of David, the Messiah, would defeat the gentile enemies. As ruler of Israel, he would be the captain of the forces that would dominate

all the nations; they would elevate Jerusalem so as to glorify the Lord. In other words, presented here is a political reign of justice in which the Messiah and Israel are the head of the entire world. The Zealots in Jesus' time had similar messianic hopes but the difference was that they themselves would establish the Kingdom by means of an armed uprising.[2]

A new prophetic voice had come to the people of Israel and the people wanted to hear his teachings. The crowd that followed and listened to Jesus were mostly the poor and those marginalized by society and the religiosity of the status quo. This prophet from Galilee identified with his listeners because of his background. When Nathanael, who would become his disciple, learned of Jesus' background and his hometown, he questioned Jesus' messianic identity.

> JOHN 1:45-46 *"Philip found Nathanael and told him, 'We have found the one Moses wrote about in the Law, and about whom the prophets also wrote—Jesus of Nazareth, the son of Joseph.'*
>
> *'Nazareth! Can anything good come from there?' Nathanael asked."*

Cut off from the rest of the country, Galilee was never an integral part of the "promised land." However, this was the region that provided a home for Jesus and his first disciples and made up his first missionary field. Prior to the Passion, the majority of the Gospel stories are situated around the vicinity of the Sea of Galilee.[3]

Jesus established a preferential relationship with the poor because he was one of them. His preaching of the Kingdom was not only out of his own human embodiment, but also in his cultural context. "He spoke with a Galilean accent; his formal education was limited; and his trade was carpentry." Theologian and missiologist Orlando E. Costas left a legacy in his classic book *Christ Outside the Gate* in presenting Jesus in his sociohistorical context for reflection on the mission of the church. One of the teachings and proclamations of Jesus about the Kingdom would be marked with a series of beatitudes for those who live under the universal reign of the Messiah.

> MATTHEW 5:1-12 *"Now when Jesus saw the crowds, he went up on a mountainside and sat down. His disciples came to him, and he began to teach them. He said:*
>
> *Blessed are the poor in spirit, for theirs is the Kingdom of heaven.*
>
> *Blessed are those who mourn, for they will be comforted.*
>
> *Blessed are the meek, for they will inherit the earth.*
>
> *Blessed are those who hunger and thirst for righteousness, for they will be filled.*
>
> *Blessed are the merciful, for they will be shown mercy.*
>
> *Blessed are the pure in heart, for they will see God.*
>
> *Blessed are the peacemakers, for they will be called children of God.*
>
> *Blessed are those who are persecuted because of righteousness, for theirs is the Kingdom of heaven.*
>
> *Blessed are you when people insult you, persecute you and falsely say all kinds of evil against you because of me. Rejoice and be glad, because great is your reward in heaven, for in the same way they persecuted the prophets who were before you."*

PREACHING AND THE MOVEMENT OF THE KINGDOM OF GOD

Jesus established the essential values of the Kingdom of God and how those who voluntarily enter into citizenship of the Kingdom should live. This Kingdom would not be like the kingdoms of the earth's kings and rulers. Jesus' teachings about the Kingdom of God would not only be about the principles and values that govern this new Kingdom and the characteristics of its citizens, it would also be accompanied by concrete manifestations that would bring physical health and freedom from demonic oppression.

> MATTHEW 15:29-31 *"Jesus left there and went along the Sea of Galilee. Then he went up on a mountainside and sat down. Great crowds came to him, bringing the lame, the blind, the crippled, the mute and many others, and laid them at his feet; and he healed them. The people were amazed when they saw the mute speaking, the crippled made well, the lame walking and the blind seeing. And they praised the God of Israel."*

The crowds followed Jesus, but he didn't expect that people would only *come* to him, he also *went* to the towns and villages to fulfill the mission of the Kingdom of God. He looked for opportunities to go.

> MATTHEW 4:23-24 *"Jesus went throughout Galilee, teaching in their synagogues, proclaiming the good news of the Kingdom, and healing every disease and sickness among the people. News about him spread all over Syria, and people brought to him all who were ill with various diseases, those suffering severe pain, the demon-possessed, those having seizures, and the paralyzed; and he healed them."*

On the day of Pentecost, the apostle Peter preached about the Messiah, the Lord and King of the universal Kingdom of God:

> Acts 2:29-30 *"Fellow Israelites, I can tell you confidently that the patriarch David died and was buried, and his tomb is here to this day. But he was a prophet and knew that God had promised him on oath that he would place one of his descendants on his throne."*

The apostles Peter and John preached that the universal Kingdom of the Messiah offered to its citizens the forgiveness of sins and eternal salvation. The King also gave them authority and power to heal the sick. When Peter and John went up to the temple at the customary time of prayer, they found a man lame from birth. They put into practice the authority of the King to heal the man:

> Acts 3:4-8 *"Peter looked straight at him, as did John. Then Peter said, 'Look at us!' So the man gave them his attention, expecting to get something from them.*
>
> *Then Peter said, 'Silver or gold I do not have, but what I do have I give you. In the name of Jesus Christ of Nazareth, walk.'*
>
> *Taking him by the right hand, he helped him up, and instantly the man's feet and ankles became strong. He jumped to his feet and began to walk. Then he went with them into the temple courts, walking and jumping, and praising God."*

Jesus disciples carried out the teachings of the good news of the Kingdom with authority and power to heal and to set free those oppressed by the devil. The manifestations of the

Kingdom were visible to those who were listening and embraced the new faith in Jesus Christ:

> ACTS 8:4-8 *"Those who had been scattered preached the word wherever they went. Philip went down to a city in Samaria and proclaimed the Messiah there. When the crowds heard Philip and saw the signs he performed, they all paid close attention to what he said. For with shrieks, impure spirits came out of many, and many who were paralyzed or lame were healed. So there was great joy in that city."*

Paul and Barnabas, called by the Holy Spirit and sent by the church in Antioch, embarked on their first missionary journey to preach the gospel of Jesus Christ. When they arrived in the city of Lystra, the health needs were obvious.

> ACTS 14:7-10 *"They continued to preach the gospel. In Lystra there sat a man who was lame. He had been that way from birth and had never walked. He listened to Paul as he was speaking. Paul looked directly at him, saw that he had faith to be healed and called out, 'Stand up on your feet!' At that, the man jumped up and began to walk."*

On his second missionary journey, Paul arrived at the city of Philippi where he announced the gospel of Jesus Christ. In that city, the book of Acts records that Paul spoke to a group of women on the Sabbath day. After that conversation, a godly woman named Lydia was converted. Paul also had to confront a fortune teller in that area.

> ACTS 16:16-18 *"Once when we were going to the place of prayer, we were met by a female slave who had a spirit by which she predicted the future. She earned a great deal of money for her owners by fortune-telling. She followed Paul*

and the rest of us, shouting, 'These men are servants of the Most High God, who are telling you the way to be saved.' She kept this up for many days. Finally Paul became so annoyed that he turned around and said to the spirit, 'In the name of Jesus Christ I command you to come out of her!' At that moment the spirit left her."

The apostle Paul had the certainty that preaching about the Kingdom came with the power of the Holy Spirit and the authority that Jesus Christ had given to his church:

> EPHESIANS 1:19-23 *"And his incomparably great power for us who believe. That power is the same as the mighty strength he exerted when he raised Christ from the dead and seated him at his right hand in the heavenly realms, far above all rule and authority, power and dominion, and every name that is invoked, not only in the present age but also in the one to come. And God placed all things under his feet and appointed him to be head over everything for the church, which is his body, the fullness of him who fills everything in every way."*

Throughout the history of the church God has called men and women to proclaim the good news of the Kingdom of God for the salvation of souls by the merits of the sacrifice of Jesus Christ. REVELATION 1:5 *"And from Jesus Christ, who is the faithful witness, the firstborn from the dead, and the ruler of the kings of the earth. To him who loves us and has freed us from our sins by his blood."* History bears witness of how God has used his servants with power and authority to manifest the works of the Kingdom in healing, wonders and setting oppressed people free from the forces of Satan.

The spiritual measure of Christian leaders is the fullness of the Spirit and its promulgation of power. The oratory, the effectiveness of the preaching of the sermon and the lexicon of speaking are good, but not good enough. The content, the orthodoxy and the solid biblical truth are essential but not enough. The personality, the grace to speak and act are important but not sufficient. The power of the Lord must be on them. ... The Kingdom should be built, advanced and expressed at the level of the divine giving power to the human being. It must be God who works through us.[4]

QUESTIONS FOR REFLECTION

1. How has this chapter about the movement of the mission and Jesus' activity in the fulfillment of the mission impacted you?
2. How have Jesus' teachings about the Beatitudes helped you?
3. What other biblical passages would you use for this chapter?
4. How have you been inspired by the apostles' proclamation of the gospel with authority and power to preach, heal, and cast out demons?
5. On a scale of 1 to 10, with 10 being the highest score, answer this question: How often do you put into practice praying for the sick?

> 2 KINGS 5:2-3 *"Now bands of raiders from Aram had gone out and had taken captive a young girl from Israel, and she served Naaman's wife. She said to her mistress, 'If only my master would see the prophet who is in Samaria! He would cure him of his leprosy.'"*

6. How can I have conviction to pray for the sick and for those who suffer from vices and addictions to be set free?

There is pow'r, pow'r, wonder working power
In the blood of the lamb.
There is pow'r, pow'r, wonder working power
In the precious blood of the Lamb.
—*Sing to the Lord, #449*

7. For further reflection on this chapter, if possible, take time to pray and study the scriptures you have found.

CHAPTER 8

VISION

> *Don't you have a saying, "It's still four months until harvest"? I tell you, open your eyes and look at the fields! They are ripe for harvest. Even now the one who reaps draws a wage and harvests a crop for eternal life, so that the sower and the reaper may be glad together. Thus the saying "One sows and another reaps" is true. I sent you to reap what you have not worked for. Others have done the hard work, and you have reaped the benefits of their labor.* (John 4:35-38)

In the narrative of the Gospel of John we read about the meeting between Jesus and the Samaritan woman. The passage describes how Jesus was looking for every opportunity to preach and minister, not only to the crowds, but also on a personal level. He saw people through Kingdom eyes in the fulfillment of the mission.

On Jesus' journey with his disciples toward Jerusalem, the Jews customarily did not pass through the city of Sychar, in Samaria, but Jesus had a plan that went against that traditional path of travel on the map.

> The narrative of the conversation between Jesus and the Samaritan woman presents certain religious and socio-cultural elements of the relationship between the Jews and the Samaritans.... "I end to state that the New Testament describes the inhabitants of Samaria, a mixed race, the result of a merger of the remnant Israelites with the gentiles that the Assyrians led to the region after the fall of Israel (722 BC)."[1]

The dialog between Jesus and the Samaritan woman is one of the most fascinating narratives in the Gospels, because Jesus breaks several of the stereotypes and religious and socio-cultural traditions of the Samaritans and Jews to evangelize the woman. A conversation between a Jew and a Samaritan woman was culturally unacceptable. Jesus broke with rabbinic protocol to present the good news of the Kingdom to a woman marginalized by her society because of her lifestyle of having had several husbands.

In his conversation with the Samaritan woman, Jesus made several declarations, offering her a new opportunity to rebuild her life. Jesus offers the woman living water. JOHN 4:14 *"But whoever drinks the water I give them will never thirst. Indeed, the water I give them will become in them a spring of water welling up to eternal life."* The Samaritan woman received the gift of eternal life of the Kingdom and immediately went back to her home to share the joy of the new life which Christ had given her. Upon hearing the woman's news the neighbors quickly left to go find Jesus and confirm if what the woman said was true, since she seemed to have spoken with the Messiah.

> JOHN 4:39-42 *"Many of the Samaritans from that town believed in him because of the woman's testimony, 'He told me everything I ever did.' So when the Samaritans came to him, they urged him to stay with them, and he stayed two days. And because of his words many more became believers.*
>
> *They said to the woman, 'We no longer believe just because of what you said; now we have heard for ourselves, and we know that this man really is the Savior of the world.'"*

Jesus accepted the invitation to stay a little longer in that city, where even the Jews avoided transit due to the cultural and religious prejudices of the time. The Master knew the invitation would give him the opportunity to fulfill the mission of preaching the good news of the Kingdom to those who were expecting the arrival of the Messiah, even though they had different teachings about the correct place to worship the God of Father Abraham's covenant. *"Believe me, a time is coming when you will worship the Father neither on this mountain nor in Jerusalem."*

After the disciples returned from buying food, Jesus exhorts them to expand their vision for the people since that area was ready to receive the message of the good news of the Kingdom. He calls to their attention that fulfilling the mission is more important than eating, and they should take advantage of every opportunity. The people of that area were ready to receive the eternal teachings of the Kingdom beyond what the disciples could even imagine.

Jesus taught his disciples that, when preaching the message of the Kingdom, they should not be exclusive or partial to anyone because of his or her race, cultural or religious beliefs. Jesus saw the needs and potential of the people, not at all like their culture or society saw them. The story of the tax collector Levi, who became one of his disciples, is another example of how Jesus looked at people with the eyes of the Kingdom:

> LUKE 5:27-32 *"After this, Jesus went out and saw a tax collector by the name of Levi sitting at his tax booth.*
>
> *'Follow me,' Jesus said to him, and Levi got up, left everything and followed him. Then Levi held a great banquet for Jesus at his house, and a large crowd of tax collectors and others were eating with them.*
>
> *But the Pharisees and the teachers of the law who belonged to their sect complained to his disciples, 'Why do you eat and drink with tax collectors and sinners?'*
>
> *Jesus answered them, 'It is not the healthy who need a doctor, but the sick. I have not come to call the righteous, but sinners to repentance.'"*

In the Gospels, Jesus teaches his vision to love and see people through the eyes of the Kingdom of God, a Kingdom that is universal although it began with the people of Israel. In several of the Gospel stories, Jesus ministers to those who were not Jewish. On one occasion two of his disciples introduced Jesus to some Greeks:

> JOHN 12:20-22 *"Now there were some Greeks among those who went up to worship at the festival. They came to Philip,*

> *who was from Bethsaida in Galilee, with a request. 'Sir,' they said, 'we would like to see Jesus.' Philip went to tell Andrew; Andrew and Philip in turn told Jesus."*

Because of his strong Jewish religious background, it took some time for the apostle Peter, even after Pentecost, to recognize and apply the teachings of the Master concerning the universality of the gospel. It was only through a supernatural experience that Peter finally learned the lesson that he should possess the Master's vision in the fulfillment of the mission. Peter testified about his experience in the house of Cornelius, a Roman centurion:

> ACTS 11:12-15 *"The Spirit told me to have no hesitation about going with them. These six brothers also went with me, and we entered the man's house. He told us how he had seen an angel appear in his house and say, 'Send to Joppa for Simon who is called Peter. He will bring you a message through which you and all your household will be saved.' As I began to speak, the Holy Spirit came on them as he had come on us at the beginning."*

The apostle Paul had received the commission from the risen Christ to preach the message of the gospel to all people and in particular to the Gentiles. ROMANS 1:16 *"For I am not ashamed of the gospel, because it is the power of God that brings salvation to everyone who believes: first to the Jew, then to the Gentile."* Paul possessed a very clear vision of the Kingdom: to take the gospel of Jesus Christ to as many place as possible.

> ACTS 16:8-10 *"So they passed by Mysia and went down to Troas. During the night Paul had a vision of a man of Macedonia standing and begging him, 'Come over to Macedonia and help us.' After Paul had seen the vision, we*

> *got ready at once to leave for Macedonia, concluding that God had called us to preach the gospel to them."*

The heroes of the faith who have impacted their communities, countries, and nations have had a clear vision of the Kingdom in the fulfillment of the mission. Some of them left their home countries to carry the good news of Jesus Christ to other places. Their motivation was a passionate vision for the eternal salvation for everyone. D. L. Moody said, "When I see the thousands of young people in line along the path of death, I feel that I fall at the feet of Jesus in prayer and tears to go and save them." John Wesley urged his pastors saying, "We live only for this: to save our own souls and of those who hear us."

> It is necessary in the fulfillment of the mission that we pastors and leaders have a vision of the reason for which we have been called. ... a clear vision of what God wants of us. The goals that we set for ourselves and everything we do must have the aim of achieving the best results.[2]

Every church needs a focus (a vision). Not just any focus, but of the Kingdom. A true focus begins with God and reaches the people whom God loves and with whom he desires to establish a relationship.[3]

QUESTIONS FOR REFLECTION

1. How has this chapter about Jesus' vision in the fulfillment of the mission impacted you?
2. Has Jesus' teaching to his disciples that the harvest is ready helped you?
3. What other biblical passages would you use for this chapter?

VISION

4. How have you been inspired by the apostles' passion and vision in the fulfillment of the mission?
5. On a scale of 1 to 10, with 10 being the highest score, answer this question: How much vision do I have to fulfill the mission?

   HABAKKUK 2:2-3 *"Then the Lord replied 'Write down the revelation and make it plain on tablets so that a herald may run with it. For the revelation awaits an appointed time; it speaks of the end and will not prove false. Though it linger, wait for it; it will certainly come and will not delay.'"*

6. How can I have a clear vision of the church's mission?

   Send the power, O Lord, Send the Power, O Lord.
   Send the Holy Ghost power, Let it now be out-poured.
   Send it surging and sweeping Like the waves of the sea.
   Send a world-wide revival, And begin it in me.
   —Hymn, "For a Worldwide Revival," cyberhymnal.org

7. For further reflection on this chapter, if possible, take time to pray and study the scriptures you have found.

CHAPTER 9

FAITH

> *A furious squall came up, and the waves broke over the boat, so that it was nearly swamped. Jesus was in the stern, sleeping on a cushion. The disciples woke him and said to him, "Teacher, don't you care if we drown?" He got up, rebuked the wind and said to the waves, "Quiet! Be still!" Then the wind died down and it was completely calm. He said to his disciples, "Why are you so afraid? Do you still have no faith?" They were terrified and asked each other, "Who is this? Even the wind and the waves obey him!" (Mark 4:37-41)*

Faith was an essential principle of Jesus' ministry in the fulfillment of the mission. His life revolved around a total dependence of believing that all things are possible by trusting the

Father Almighty. ᴸᵁᴷᴱ ¹⁸:²⁷ *"Jesus replied, 'What is impossible with man is possible with God.'"* Jesus' faith was sourced from the Creator of the universe. The God who made the heavens and the earth and all existence had sent him on his mission, and he had the conviction that God the Father supported him.

Nature would be subject to Jesus as the author of Hebrews states: *"But in these last days he has spoken to us by his Son, whom he appointed heir of all things, and through whom also he made the universe."* Jesus performed miracles because he had the power of the Holy Spirit in his life and complete certainty in the Father who had made him heir of all creation.

Jesus moved in the world with supernatural faith to do miracles in the fulfillment of the mission, giving sight to the blind, healing lepers, making the lame to walk, casting out demons, feeding the crowds, turning water into wine and resurrecting the dead. Jesus performed all the miracles because of his total faith in the Father.

> ᴹᴬᵀᵀᴴᴱᵂ ¹⁴:²⁵⁻³¹ *"Shortly before dawn Jesus went out to them, walking on the lake. When the disciples saw him walking on the lake, they were terrified. 'It's a ghost,' they said, and cried out in fear.*
>
> *But Jesus immediately said to them: 'Take courage! It is I. Don't be afraid.'*
>
> *'Lord, if it's you,' Peter replied, 'tell me to come to you on the water.'*
>
> *'Come,' he said. Then Peter got down out of the boat, walked on the water and came toward Jesus.*

FAITH

> *But when he saw the wind, he was afraid and, beginning to sink, cried out, 'Lord, save me!' Immediately Jesus reached out his hand and caught him.*
>
> *'You of little faith,' he said, 'why did you doubt?'"*

Jesus also wanted his disciples to exercise faith and continually exhorted them to have faith as a fundamental essential for the accomplishment of the mission. Peter's fear made him doubt and not have faith that the Master had control over the turbulent waters troubled by the wind. The Master granted Peter's request to walk on the water, then to take care of him and not let him drown.

The apostles were learning their lesson of faith by seeing that the Master's life was governed and directed by total security and trust in the Father. They wanted to have faith like the Master and requested. LUKE 17:5-6 *"The apostles said to the Lord, 'Increase our faith!' He replied, 'If you have faith as small as a mustard seed, you can say to this mulberry tree, 'Be uprooted and planted in the sea,' and it will obey you.'"* Jesus told them that they should believe in him for the foundation of their faith: *"Very truly I tell you, whoever believes in me will do the works I have been doing, and they will do even greater things than these, because I am going to the Father."*

Jesus' faith was molded not only by the great miracles he did, but also by his daily life, trusting that God would provide for his most basic needs in the fulfillment of the mission. Jesus taught his disciples a basic lesson of faith which was to rely on the provision of the Father through this illustration.

MATTHEW 6:25-33 *"Therefore I tell you, do not worry about your life, what you will eat or drink; or about your body,*

> *what you will wear. Is not life more than food, and the body more than clothes? Look at the birds of the air; they do not sow or reap or store away in barns, and yet your heavenly Father feeds them. Are you not much more valuable than they? Can any one of you by worrying add a single hour to your life? And why do you worry about clothes? See how the flowers of the field grow. They do not labor or spin. Yet I tell you that not even Solomon in all his splendor was dressed like one of these. If that is how God clothes the grass of the field, which is here today and tomorrow is thrown into the fire, will he not much more clothe you—you of little faith? So do not worry, saying, 'What shall we eat?' or 'What shall we drink?' or 'What shall we wear?' For the pagans run after all these things, and your heavenly Father knows that you need them. But seek first his Kingdom and his righteousness, and all these things will be given to you as well."*

When Jesus sent the seventy disciples to preach the gospel of the Kingdom, they were assured that they would have what was necessary in the fulfillment of the mission.

> LUKE 10:4-7 *"Do not take a purse or bag or sandals; and do not greet anyone on the road. 'When you enter a house, first say, 'Peace to this house.' If someone who promotes peace is there, your peace will rest on them; if not, it will return to you. Stay there, eating and drinking whatever they give you, for the worker deserves his wages. Do not move around from house to house."*

The church's foundation was faith and was essential for its life and doctrine. ACTS 16:5 *"So the churches were strengthened in the faith and grew daily in numbers."* The life of the disciples and of the church would be established through faith in the gospel of Jesus Christ. ROMANS 1:17 *"For in the gospel the righteousness of God is*

FAITH

revealed—a righteousness that is by faith from first to last, just as it is written: "The righteous will live by faith."

In the salutation of his final letter to the Philippians, the apostle Paul calls them to have faith in God the provider.

> PHILIPPIANS 4:19-20 *"And my God will meet all your needs according to the riches of his glory in Christ Jesus. To our God and Father be glory for ever and ever. Amen."*

Paul based his life on the principle of faith and recommended that the church in Corinth, in his second letter, live and move by faith.

> 2 CORINTHIANS 5:6-7 *"Therefore we are always confident and know that as long as we are at home in the body we are away from the Lord. For we live by faith, not by sight."*

In Hebrews, the writer begins with a definition of faith to introduce the heroes of faith from the Old Testament, which should serve as an inspiration for Christians to live in total confidence in the author of the faith, Jesus Christ.

> HEBREWS 11:1-3 *"Now faith is confidence in what we hope for and assurance about what we do not see. This is what the ancients were commended for. By faith we understand that the universe was formed at God's command, so that what is seen was not made out of what was visible."*

> HEBREWS 12:1-2 *"Therefore, since we are surrounded by such a great cloud of witnesses, let us throw off everything that hinders and the sin that so easily entangles. And let us run with perseverance the race marked out for us, fixing our eyes on Jesus, the pioneer and perfecter of faith. For the joy set before him he endured the cross, scorning its shame, and sat down at the right hand of the throne of God."*

FULFILLING THE MISSION

Throughout the history of the church, God has raised up a new cloud of heroes of the faith who put all their trust in Jesus Christ under the power and direction of the Holy Spirit. The testimonies of the works done by them in the name of the author and perfecter of faith, have marked the transformation of thousands and thousands of men and women redeemed by faith in Jesus Christ. Continents, countries, cities, neighborhoods, and communities have been transformed by the faithful obedience of these men and women of faith, who believed in God as they fulfilled the mission.

> Is there anything that encircles more mystery or greater usefulness than a key? The mystery: "Why is it there? What can it set into motion? What will it open? What new discovery could it motivate?" The usefulness: "It *has* to open something, without a doubt, someone owns it! It must *decipher* something, with its security, and it could give rise to a possibility that would otherwise be empty!" The "keys" are concepts, biblical themes, which can be traced through the Scriptures and verified when applied with a faith well established under the lordship of Jesus Christ." [1]

QUESTIONS FOR REFLECTION

1. How has this chapter about Jesus' faith for the fulfillment of the mission impacted you?
2. How have Jesus' teachings to his disciples about faith helped you?
3. What other biblical passages would you use for this chapter?
4. Have you been inspired by the apostles' faith in the fulfillment of the mission? If yes, how?

FAITH

5. On a scale of 1 to 10, with 10 being the highest score, answer this question: How much faith do I have in fulfilling the mission?

   2 CHRONICLES 20:19-20 *"Then some Levites from the Kohathites and Korahites stood up and praised the Lord, the God of Israel, with a very loud voice. Early in the morning they left for the Desert of Tekoa. As they set out, Jehoshaphat stood and said, 'Listen to me, Judah and people of Jerusalem! Have faith in the Lord your God and you will be upheld; have faith in his prophets and you will be successful.'"*

6. How can I increase my faith?

   Living by faith, in Jesus above;
   Trusting, confiding in His great love;
   Safe from all harm in His sheltering arm,
   I'm living by faith and feel no alarm.

   —*Sing to the Lord #566*

7. For further reflection on this chapter, if possible, take time to pray and study the scriptures you have found.

CHAPTER 10

COMPASSION

> *When Jesus landed and saw a large crowd, he had compassion on them, because they were like sheep without a shepherd. So he began teaching them many things. By this time it was late in the day, so his disciples came to him. 'This is a remote place,' they said, 'and it's already very late. Send the people away so that they can go to the surrounding countryside and villages and buy themselves something to eat.' But he answered, 'You give them something to eat.'"* (Mark 6:34-37)

Jesus had a compassionate heart for people and made them a priority in order to meet their needs. He was willing to change his agenda so he could minister to the crowds that followed him. In the context of the passage above, the disciples had returned from a tour of preaching about the Kingdom of God. After listening to the their reports of their experiences, Jesus invited them to relax. When they landed they found a huge crowd ready to listen to the Master's teachings, so the time of resting had to be modified in order to respond to the crowd, which was doing everything possible to hear Jesus' message.

Although it is not mentioned in the passage, it was probable that Jesus healed the sick and freed those who were possessed by unclean spirits, since that was a common activity for his mission. Hours passed and the people were captivated by the Master's ministry; the day was ending. The disciples assisted Jesus with some details of his ministry and, on this occasion, they had to tell the Master it was time to dismiss the crowd.

Jesus was aware that the crowd had traveled from different places and spent a long time listening to the eternal truths of the Kingdom, and, because of this, he did not want to dismiss the crowd without feeding them before they returned to their homes. He told his disciples to feed the crowd. The disciples were surprised by such a request because it was humanly impossible to provide that much food for that great multitude of five thousand men, not counting the women and children.

The disciples who responded to Jesus' command of, *"Give them something to eat,"* found five loaves of bread and two fish, which they took to the Master. Those few loaves and fish, obviously, were not enough to feed the multitude, but in the hands of the Master, it was enough to more than satisfy everyone. After everyone had eaten there was plenty leftover, enough to fill 12 baskets.

COMPASSION

On that occasion Jesus established the principle that his disciples would be responsible for responding with compassion when they saw people in need. Preaching the good news of the Kingdom would be paired with having compassion to feed the hungry and help the needy.

> MATTHEW 25:34-40 *"Then the King will say to those on his right, 'Come, you who are blessed by my Father; take your inheritance, the Kingdom prepared for you since the creation of the world. For I was hungry and you gave me something to eat, I was thirsty and you gave me something to drink, I was a stranger and you invited me in, I needed clothes and you clothed me, I was sick and you looked after me, I was in prison and you came to visit me.'*
>
> *Then the righteous will answer him, 'Lord, when did we see you hungry and feed you, or thirsty and give you something to drink? When did we see you a stranger and invite you in, or needing clothes and clothe you? When did we see you sick or in prison and go to visit you?'*
>
> *The King will reply, 'Truly I tell you, whatever you did for one of the least of these brothers and sisters of mine, you did for me.'"*

The disciples learned the principle of compassion in the fulfillment of the mission and established compassion as a lifestyle in the early church. They would care for the most needy:

> ACTS 2:44-45 *"All the believers were together and had everything in common. They sold property and possessions to give to anyone who had need."*

The apostle Paul calls on the church in Ephesus to practice a new lifestyle in Jesus Christ by being generous with the needy.

FULFILLING THE MISSION

EPHESIANS 4:28 *"Anyone who has been stealing must steal no longer, but must work, doing something useful with their own hands, that they may have something to share with those in need."* The apostle James exhorts the church to do works of charity. JAMES 2:15-17 *"Suppose a brother or a sister is without clothes and daily food. If one of you says to them, 'Go in peace; keep warm and well fed,' but does nothing about their physical needs, what good is it? In the same way, faith by itself, if it is not accompanied by action, is dead."*

Throughout history and since its beginning, the church of Jesus Christ has been characterized by Jesus' compassion, which is a large and integral part of the message in the fulfillment of the mission. Throughout its history, Christians have established hospitals, clinics, schools, orphanages, and feeding centers in their faithfulness to Jesus' teachings of, *"Give them something to eat."*

> We, the Wesleyans, are a united group but not a closed family. Our heritage is a family united by the power of love, who always tries to reach out to others with compassion and with open arms to bring into the circle new people, different, and deprived of their rights.[1]

In its formative years, the Church of the Nazarene practiced Jesus' compassion. In the book *Our Watchword & Song*, the writer declares,

> We maintain the ministry of compassion as a response to the material needs of the world. The Nazarenes maintained several orphanages, maternity homes, houses of refuge…[2]

> As people devoted to God, we share his love for the lost and his compassion for the poor and the afflicted. The Greatest Commandment (Matthew 22:36-40) and the Great Commission

COMPASSION

(Matthew 28:19-20) compel us to confront the world with evangelism, compassion and justice.[3]

The mission statement of Compassionate Ministries in the USA/Canada Region states the following.

> Nazarene Compassionate Ministries (NCM) seeks to live and act compassionately in the world following Christ's own life and ministry. We seek to be incarnations of the same gospel that Christ lived and preached and to be witnesses to the same love and compassion God has for our world. In the United States and Canada, NCM works closely with Compassionate Ministry Centers (CMCs) to bring compassion and healing to communities that need the love and presence of Christ.
>
> We believe that every follower of Jesus is called to be compassion to their community. Since the earliest days of the church, Christians have been involved in ministry to the marginalized all over the world. The Church of the Nazarene specifically has affirmed the need for the church to embrace those who have been ignored by society. This charge is not just institutional; it is a personal call on the life of every Christian.[4]

QUESTIONS FOR REFLECTION

1. How has this chapter about Jesus' compassion in the fulfillment of the mission impacted you?
2. How have Jesus' teachings to his disciples about compassion helped you?
3. What other biblical passages would you use for this chapter?
4. How has the church's life of compassion in the fulfillment of the mission inspired you?

5. On a scale of 1 to 10, with 10 being the highest score, answer this question: Do you practice Jesus' compassion in the fulfillment of the mission?

   MICAH 6:8 *"He has shown you, O mortal, what is good. And what does the Lord require of you? To act justly and to love mercy and to walk humbly with your God."*

6. How can I have a compassionate heart?

   We'll girdle the globe with salvation,
   With holiness unto the Lord;
   And light shall illumine each nation,
   The light from the lamp of His Word.
   —*"We'll Girdle the Globe," cyberhymnal.org*

7. For further reflection on this chapter, if possible, take time to pray and study the scriptures you have found.

CHAPTER 11

ORGANIZATION

"

About five thousand men were there. But he said to his disciples, "Have them sit down in groups of about fifty each." The disciples did so, and everyone sat down. Taking the five loaves and the two fish and looking up to heaven, he gave thanks and broke them. Then he gave them to the disciples to distribute to the people. They all ate and were satisfied, and the disciples picked up twelve basketfuls of broken pieces that were left over. (Luke 9:14-17)

"

In the miracle event of multiplying the loaves and fish to feed the multitude of listeners, Jesus used the principle of organization. He was an excellent manager of the resources he had at his disposal. He organized the disciples two by two when he sent them out to preach the news of the Kingdom; he applied the counsel of the writer of the book of Ecclesiastes:

> ECCLESIASTES 4:9-10 *"Two are better than one, because they have a good return for their labor: If either of them falls down, one can help the other up. But pity anyone who falls and has no one to help them up."*

Not only did he organize them two by two, he also considered the personality of each one of the disciples to make the teams. This team relationship continued even after his ascension. ACTS 3:1 *"One day Peter and John were going up to the temple at the time of prayer—at three in the afternoon."*

Being sent in pairs would help the disciples on their long journeys and give them better protection against the risks and dangers of the trips. The mutual support and fellowship helped them get to their destinations. These trips required a system of organization to allocate and distribute the routes where Jesus was sending them. This could not be done randomly or spontaneously. Jesus designed an evangelistic plan and optimized their resources to reach the greatest number of cities and thus reach the greatest number of people.

Jesus shows his organizational abilities not only by sending his disciples in pairs, but also by training and giving them specific instructions as to how they should enter houses, how to behave in response to the reactions of others, and how they should respond to generosity and hospitality. Without a doubt, Jesus devoted time for strategic training and organization to achieve greater effectiveness in fulfilling the mission.

> Many have spoken and written about Jesus as a preacher, miracle-worker, teacher, and other important facets of his grand

ORGANIZATION

personality. Few have discovered him as a chief executive officer and administrative leader who knew how to recruit, train, inspire, motivate, and lead a team of twelve men who, under his influence and direction and in accordance with his plans and objectives, conquered the world for his cause.[1]

Jesus gave his disciples specific instructions in preparation for the festivities that would conclude his messianic mission, the triumphal entry into Jerusalem. Jesus outlined an organizational plan for this event:

> MARK 11:1-2 *"As they approached Jerusalem and came to Bethphage and Bethany at the Mount of Olives, Jesus sent two of his disciples, saying to them, 'Go to the village ahead of you, and just as you enter it, you will find a colt tied there, which no one has ever ridden. Untie it and bring it here.'"*

Another influential event in Jesus' life and ministry was the Passover feast, the Last Supper, with his disciples. This feast would require detailed planning in accordance with the historic traditions of the celebration. Jesus instructed his disciples so that not one element or tradition was overlooked in the Passover meal as this is where he would affirm God's plan for the new covenant of salvation for the human race.

> MATTHEW 26:17-19 *"On the first day of the Festival of Unleavened Bread, the disciples came to Jesus and asked, 'Where do you want us to make preparations for you to eat the Passover?' He replied, 'Go into the city to a certain man and tell him, 'The Teacher says: My appointed time is near. I am going to celebrate the Passover with my disciples at your house.' So the disciples did as Jesus had directed them and prepared the Passover."*

The apostles learned the principle of organization from the Master and implemented it in the fulfillment of the mission. The book of Acts records the aspects of this organizational structure in the first years of the early church. The fishermen of Galilee are now the senior leaders of the church of Jesus Christ and have to provide administrative and organizational direction for the distribution of goods with the new community of faith. The selection of the first deacons to serve the widows reveals the disciples' abilities to establish a new structured committee that would resolve the tension emerging among the community of the first believers:

> ACTS 6:2-3 *"So the Twelve gathered all the disciples together and said, 'It would not be right for us to neglect the ministry of the word of God in order to wait on tables. Brothers and sisters, choose seven men from among you who are known to be full of the Spirit and wisdom. We will turn this responsibility over to them.'"*

The apostles had learned by watching the way Jesus organized and delegated specific tasks to his disciples in the fulfillment of the mission of the Kingdom. The explosive growth of the early church would require more delegation to new leaders in order to sustain the exponential growth of those days.

> ACTS 6:7 *"So the word of God spread. The number of disciples in Jerusalem increased rapidly, and a large number of priests became obedient to the faith."*

Directed by the Holy Spirit, the church in Antioch organized the first group of missionaries in the fulfillment of the mission. They would send Barnabas and Paul to expand the borders of the Kingdom of God beyond their city. Although it

ORGANIZATION

was an act guided by the Holy Spirit, it still needed an organizational structure for sending these first missionaries. Paul used the principle of strategic organization to establish and advance the mission of the church through a strategic plan to go to the cities.

> ACTS 18:22-23 *"When he landed at Caesarea, he went up to Jerusalem and greeted the church and then went down to Antioch. After spending some time in Antioch, Paul set out from there and traveled from place to place throughout the region of Galatia and Phrygia, strengthening all the disciples."*

In their first missionary tour, Paul and Barnabas organized the new believers: *"[They] appointed elders for them in each church."* Organization and structure were fundamental in supporting the establishment of the new churches in the Kingdom of God.

John Wesley, a man anointed by the Holy Spirit with the passion of an apostle for souls, understood the virtue of using the principle of organization. He organized leaders and members of his movement into groups, bands, classes, and societies that would effectively establish and develop the people called "Methodists." Wesley's strategic organizational genius was in the formation of these small groups for evangelism and discipleship. He would tell his leaders: "Preach in as many places as possible. Organize as many classes as possible, but do not preach without organizing new classes."

George Whitefield said, "My brother, Wesley, was wiser than I. He organized the souls who were converted under his ministry into classes. I was careless and my people have become like sand that is gone with the wind." Without a doubt, Wesley's organizational and administrative ability helped him sustain the movement that God put in his hands to evangelize England and the world.

> A good executive delegates, cares for, and is surrounded by the best possible team, which allows him to fulfill his obligations and carry out all the work of the company in the best way.²

QUESTIONS FOR REFLECTION

1. How has this chapter on the use of organization in the fulfillment of the mission impacted you?
2. How have Jesus' teachings about organization helped you?
3. What other biblical passages would you use for this chapter?
4. How has the use of organization by the apostles in the fulfillment of the mission helped you?
5. On a scale of 1 to 10, with 10 being the highest score, answer this question: Do I use the principle of organization in the fulfillment of the mission?

> EXODUS 18:17-21) *"Moses' father-in-law replied, 'What you are doing is not good. You and these people who come to you will only wear yourselves out. The work is too heavy for you; you cannot handle it alone. Listen now to me and I will give you some advice, and may God be with you. You must be the people's representative before God and bring their disputes to him. Teach them his decrees and instructions, and show them the way they are to live and how they are to behave. But select capable men from all the people—men who fear God, trustworthy men who hate dishonest gain—and appoint them as officials over thousands, hundreds, fifties and tens."*

ORGANIZATION

6. How can I use organization?

   Our field is the Hispanic America,
   A young, chosen and hardworking people.
   Let us all work together today… (literal translation).
   —*Spanish Hymnal, Gracia y Devoción #344*

7. For further reflection on this chapter, if possible, take time to pray and study the scriptures you have found.

CHAPTER 12

REST AND SPIRITUAL RETREAT

"

The apostles gathered around Jesus and reported to him all they had done and taught. Then, because so many people were coming and going that they did not even have a chance to eat, he said to them, "Come with me by yourselves to a quiet place and get some rest." So they went away by themselves in a boat to a solitary place. (Mark 6:30-32)

"

Upon their return, the disciples gave the Master an account of what they had done while on their journey of preaching the good news of the Kingdom. Jesus was aware of the amount of physical and emotional energy it took to fulfill the mission.

Jesus cared for his disciples and had planned to retreat with them to rest and recover their strength after the missionary tour. His invitation to his disciples to come and rest for a while shows us how vital rest is for the human body.

The God of creation rested after all his work of creating the heavens and the earth. It was not that God needed rest. Rather, he was establishing the principle of setting aside time to rest and teaching the human race that rest is an essential part of the pace of everyday life:

> GENESIS 2:1-3 *"Thus the heavens and the earth were completed in all their vast array. By the seventh day God had finished the work he had been doing; so on the seventh day he rested from all his work. Then God blessed the seventh day and made it holy, because on it he rested from all the work of creating that he had done."*

Centuries after creation, the Hebrews were enslaved and forced to constantly yield to the demands of the Egyptian empire. Work, work, more work, more hours; the supervisors demanded more, more production; push, push, push, results, results, results. There was no rest for the slaves; their purpose was to produce for their masters. On the way to the Promised Land, God would give the commandment of the Sabbath or *shabbat* as an integral part of the rhythm of life for the people of Israel. Under the yoke of the injustice of slavery, there was no break from work, but freedom in the Promised Land had to be different. God designed rest to be necessary and right for the human body. The Sabbath would be a day of rest from daily work and labor.

REST AND SPIRITUAL RETREAT

> EXODUS 20:8-11 *"Remember the Sabbath day by keeping it holy. Six days you shall labor and do all your work, but the seventh day is a sabbath to the Lord your God. On it you shall not do any work, neither you, nor your son or daughter, nor your male or female servant, nor your animals, nor any foreigner residing in your towns. For in six days the Lord made the heavens and the earth, the sea, and all that is in them, but he rested on the seventh day. Therefore the Lord blessed the Sabbath day and made it holy."*

Horace Cowan describes the origins of the word *shabbat* in his book, *The Sabbath in Scripture and History*. He said:

> The Sabbath is not related to a number or to the duration of any period of time; it simply means to rest or cease. While Saturday is generally associated with the seventh day, it does not mean seven nor is it limited to a certain day.[1]

Jesus made sure to set aside time to rest as he ministered to the crowds and to the individuals who came to see him, as well as on travel days to cities and neighboring towns. A time to rest became an essential part of Jesus' life with his disciples. The Gospels state that Jesus retreated to deserted places to spend time with the Father. This time of retreat gave Jesus much needed rest from his ministerial duties and time to renew his physical strength. "Jesus' motivation for all he did was to save the world. He knew that he must go to his Father frequently to rest and restore his heart, mind, and fatigued body."[2] Retreating to quiet places was a consistent practice of Jesus, and he used it to train his disciples.

> MATTHEW 17:1-2 *"After six days Jesus took with him Peter, James and John the brother of James, and led them up a high*

mountain by themselves. There he was transfigured before them. His face shone like the sun, and his clothes became as white as the light."

That retreat with three of the disciples from his intimate circle was a fresh and glorious experience in Jesus' life, one where he received affirmation of the Father's satisfaction with his Son. This retreat would be unforgettable for the apostle Peter, who makes reference to this time years later in his letter to the church:

> 2 PETER 1:16-18 *"For we did not follow cleverly devised stories when we told you about the coming of our Lord Jesus Christ in power, but we were eyewitnesses of his majesty. He received honor and glory from God the Father when the voice came to him from the Majestic Glory, saying, 'This is my Son, whom I love; with him I am well pleased.' We ourselves heard this voice that came from heaven when we were with him on the sacred mountain.'"*

The apostles and their disciples would follow the example of the Master's teaching to devote time to retreat and seek the presence of the glorious Christ and to rest from the pace of the work of ministry. The principle of rest and spiritual retreat, to go and search for the presence of God, must be an important part of the lives of the men and women God calls into the ministry.

Go to the desert! Go often! The ministry you carry out is important. Your vision for God's work is significant. The calling that burns in you is urgent; but equally important, significant and urgent is God calling you: **Go to the desert! Go often!**[3]

REST AND SPIRITUAL RETREAT

QUESTIONS FOR REFLECTION

1. How has this chapter about how Jesus used rest and spiritual retreat in fulfilling the mission impacted you?
2. What have you learned about Jesus' teachings of rest and retreat?
3. What other biblical passages would you use for this chapter?
4. How has the experience of rest and spiritual retreat by the apostles in the fulfillment of the mission helped you?
5. On a scale of 1 to 10, with 10 being the highest score, answer this question: Do you take and observe a day of rest? Do you make time for spiritual retreat in the fulfillment of the mission?

   NUMBERS 10:33 *"So they set out from the mountain of the Lord and traveled for three days. The ark of the covenant of the Lord went before them during those three days to find them a place to rest."*

6. How can I maintain the discipline of finding time for rest and spiritual retreat?

   In shady green pastures so rich and so sweet,
   God leads His dear children along.
   Where the water's cool flow bathes the weary one's feet,
   God leads His dear children along.
   —*Sing to the Lord #92*

7. For further reflection on this chapter, if possible, take time to pray and study the scriptures you have found.

CHAPTER 13

THE SERVANT AND HUMILITY

"

A dispute also arose among them as to which of them was considered to be greatest. Jesus said to them, "The kings of the Gentiles Lord it over them; and those who exercise authority over them call themselves Benefactors. But you are not to be like that. Instead, the greatest among you should be like the youngest, and the one who rules like the one who serves. For who is greater, the one who is at the table or the one who serves? Is it not the one who is at the table? But I am among you as one who serves." (Luke 22:24-27)

"

Jesus modeled the principles of servanthood and humility in the fulfillment of the mission. He always taught by example. His leadership was characterized by the heart of a servant, one who served the people to whom he was ministering. He showed that there is a marked difference between a leader in the Kingdom and earthly leaders.

The principles of "authority" in the Kingdom are different from those governing earthly authorities. Jesus wanted to make sure that his disciples had a clear understanding about how they were to lead, that a position of authority is only in relation to their service in the mission. The attitude of a servant in the Kingdom must always be focused on benefiting the cause of the mission and not for personal interests, as do earthly leaders.

> MATTHEW 20:26-27 *"Not so with you. Instead, whoever wants to become great among you must be your servant, and whoever wants to be first must be your slave."*

Jesus took advantage of every opportunity to teach his disciples the principles and values of the Kingdom. Jesus' life of being a servant was consistent. At the Last Supper, before he would give himself over as the suffering servant for the redemption of the human race, he gave them a practical lesson on the attitude of a servant.

> JOHN 13:4-5 *"So he got up from the meal, took off his outer clothing, and wrapped a towel around his waist. After that, he poured water into a basin and began to wash his disciples' feet, drying them with the towel that was wrapped around him."*

Washing feet was a common custom in Jesus' time, and it was assigned to the servants or slaves of the house. Not only was it the work of the servant, but it was assigned to the servant with the lowest rank in the house. When he used the towel to wash their feet, Jesus showed his disciples how they should behave as leaders of the Kingdom, by serving those who are under their authority.

Jesus' exemplary attitude was a call to his disciples to a life of service in the fulfillment of the mission. JOHN 13:15-16 *"I have set you an example that you should do as I have done for you. Very truly I tell you, no servant is greater than his master, nor is a messenger greater than the one who sent him."* Every time the disciples were eager for and showed ambitions for power and authority, Jesus gave them a lesson on how to handle power and authority in the service of the Kingdom.

> MATTHEW 18:1-5 *"At that time the disciples came to Jesus and asked, 'Who, then, is the greatest in the Kingdom of heaven?' He called a little child to him, and placed the child among them. And he said: 'Truly I tell you, unless you change and become like little children, you will never enter the Kingdom of heaven. Therefore, whoever takes the lowly position of this child is the greatest in the Kingdom of heaven. And whoever welcomes one such child in my name welcomes me.'"*

Jesus not only demonstrated the heart and attitude of a servant by his example, he also lived the principle of humility. Even though he had the right as Lord of the world to be served with all the privileges of earthly kings, he never exercised it. His birth in a manger could not better illustrate the humility of the sovereign King when comparing his life with the kings of this world. His triumphant, messianic entry into Jerusalem mounted on a donkey was an expression of his humility.

FULFILLING THE MISSION

> **MATTHEW 21:1-5** *"As they approached Jerusalem and came to Bethphage on the Mount of Olives, Jesus sent two disciples, saying to them, 'Go to the village ahead of you, and at once you will find a donkey tied there, with her colt by her. Untie them and bring them to me. If anyone says anything to you, say that the Lord needs them, and he will send them right away.' This took place to fulfill what was spoken through the prophet: 'Say to Daughter Zion, See, your king comes to you, gentle and riding on a donkey, and on a colt, the foal of a donkey.'"*

The crowds sought and followed Jesus because he gave them confidence to approach him. They could see the transparency of his love, the humility of his heart, that of a servant. "People could feel that Jesus loved being with them. Even small children wanted to be near him, which says a lot about the kind of person he was."[1]

The apostle Paul was a man with many virtues: linguistic talents, intellectual abilities, religious achievements, and "successful" in the advancement and establishment of the church in the gentile world. All this could have caused him to have a proud attitude, but he knew that the principle of humility must be a characteristic of the people of the Kingdom, which Christ had taught by his own example.

> **2 CORINTHIANS 10:1** *"By the humility and gentleness of Christ, I appeal to you—I, Paul, who am 'timid' when face to face with you."*

Paul calls the church at Philippi to follow the example of Jesus Christ, to live with a heart of a servant and humility so that it would characterize their behavior and attitudes as followers of Christ.

THE SERVANT AND HUMILITY

> PHILIPPIANS 2:5-8 *"In your relationships with one another, have the same mindset as Christ Jesus: Who, being in very nature God, did not consider equality with God something to be used to his own advantage; rather, he made himself nothing by taking the very nature of a servant, being made in human likeness. And being found in appearance as a man, he humbled himself by becoming obedient to death—even death on a cross!"*

In his letter to the church, the apostle James advised the people to adopt an attitude of humility, quoting the psalmist: JAMES 4:6 *"But he gives us more grace. That is why Scripture says: 'God opposes the proud but shows favor to the humble.'"* Humility should be a distinguishing feature of leaders in the church of Jesus Christ in contrast with the attitudes of the arrogant leaders of the world.

> Pride makes us egocentric and leads us to think that we have a right to everything we can see, touch, or imagine. It creates greedy appetites to want more than what we need. We can be delivered from our egocentric desires when we humble ourselves before God, aware that the only thing we need is his approval.[2]

Servants of God who live with the values of the Kingdom, with a heart of servanthood and humility, attract people in the fulfillment of the mission. These leaders inspire by their example of service and humility in contrast with leaders who assume a proud attitude contrary to the characteristics of the exemplary life of the Master to his disciples.

> Christian leadership is fundamentally different from all other leadership. Even when the organization is similar to a secular organization, it will be different, by means of the Spirit of God that works in the heart, life, and leadership of the person full of

grace. By the grace of God, leaders are transformed from the inside out. This change of heart is the expression of the qualities and the likeness of Christ.³

QUESTIONS FOR REFLECTION

1. How has this chapter describing Jesus' heart of a servant and his humility in fulfilling the mission impacted you?
2. What have you learned about Jesus' teachings of the attitude of a servant and humility?
3. What other biblical passages would you use for this chapter?
4. Have you been inspired by the apostles in the fulfillment of the mission with respect to servanthood and humility?
5. On a scale of 1 to 10, with 10 being the highest score, answer this question: Do you have a life of servanthood and humility that can fulfill the mission?

   ISAIAH 66:2 *"'Has not my hand made all these things, and so they came into being?' declares the Lord. 'These are the ones I look on with favor: those who are humble and contrite in spirit, and who tremble at my word.'"*

6. How can I maintain a life of a servant and of humility?

   Thrones may fall and crumble;
   Kingdoms may rise and fall;
   But the throne of Emmanuel shall flourish above them all.
   Hallelujah!

   —*"He Shall Reign," fbcradio.org*

7. For further reflection on this chapter, if possible, take time to pray and study the scriptures you have found.

CHAPTER 14

THE COST OF SERVING

"

As they were walking along the road, a man said to him, "I will follow you wherever you go." Jesus replied, "Foxes have dens and birds have nests, but the Son of Man has no place to lay his head." He said to another man, "Follow me." But he replied, "Lord, first let me go and bury my father." Jesus said to him, "Let the dead bury their own dead, but you go and proclaim the Kingdom of God." Still another said, "I will follow you, Lord; but first let me go back and say goodbye to my family." Jesus replied, "No one who puts a hand to the plow and looks back is fit for service in the Kingdom of God."' (Luke 9:57-62)

"

Jesus paid the ultimate price by giving his life for the redemption of the human race. His life and suffering were anticipated by the prophets of God, men who gave their lives in faithful obedience to fulfill the mission of God. The prophet Isaiah announced the cost the Messiah would pay.

> Isaiah 53:5-6 *"But he was pierced for our transgressions, he was crushed for our iniquities; the punishment that brought us peace was on him, and by his wounds we are healed. We all, like sheep, have gone astray, each of us has turned to our own way; and the Lord has laid on him the iniquity of us all."*

Jesus was very clear with his disciples what it would cost to follow him and to be aware of the cost of the calling. He warned them that the calling of a disciple was not an easy road; they would run the risk of paying the price with death.

> Luke 9:23-24 *"Then he said to them all: 'Whoever wants to be my disciple must deny themselves and take up their cross daily and follow me. For whoever wants to save their life will lose it, but whoever loses their life for me will save it."*

Jesus had a simple lifestyle, limited to basic daily necessities. He prepared his disciples by example and taught what he lived. He was fed up with the inconsistency of the religious leaders and constantly confronted them because they were not prepared to do what they taught and demanded of the people. Jesus wanted to make sure that his disciples would live in accordance with the principles of his teachings and not as religious leaders.

> Matthew 23:2-4 *"The teachers of the law and the Pharisees sit in Moses' seat. So you must be careful to do everything they tell you. But do not do what they do, for they do not*

> *practice what they preach. They tie up heavy, cumbersome loads and put them on other people's shoulders, but they themselves are not willing to lift a finger to move them."*

The King of kings did not even have a house to live in let alone a palace with all the comforts and pleasures where he could entertain his disciples and followers. He chose the itinerant life and stayed in places where he met the hospitality and generosity of those who invited him in and wanted to listen to him.

In order to maintain his focus on fulfilling the mission of the Kingdom and having total dependence on the Father's provision, Jesus did not accumulate wealth or prioritize earthly, material things. Jesus was shaping his disciples to live with the priorities and values of the Kingdom and not become interested in earthly values.

> MATTHEW 6:33 *"But seek first his Kingdom and his righteousness, and all these things will be given to you as well."*

Jesus gave a series of teachings regarding the dangers of worldly riches, which can trap and corrupt people's hearts, even those who are called to serve God. MATTHEW 6:24 *"No one can serve two masters. Either you will hate the one and love the other, or you will be devoted to the one and despise the other. You cannot serve both God and money."* The Master teacher was preparing his disciples in anticipation of the life that awaited them, a life of complete dedication to their calling. He constantly talked to them about the high cost of being his disciples. He did not want his disciples to be surprised by the difficulties, persecutions and trials they would have in fulfilling the mission.

FULFILLING THE MISSION

> MATTHEW 10:16-19 *"I am sending you out like sheep among wolves. Therefore be as shrewd as snakes and as innocent as doves. Be on your guard; you will be handed over to the local councils and be flogged in the synagogues. On my account you will be brought before governors and kings as witnesses to them and to the Gentiles. But when they arrest you, do not worry about what to say or how to say it. At that time you will be given what to say."*

Jesus' apostles and the first disciples were persecuted, imprisoned, and even suffered death. That was the high cost the early church paid for being faithful to the Master's call. The Master had warned his disciples of martyrdom, imprisonments, persecutions, and other sufferings and trials to come. But, he also promised them the Holy Spirit, who would stay with them to strengthen and help them in the fulfillment of the mission by bearing witness to the glorious and victorious Christ. The book of Acts and the writings of the New Testament give testimony to the high cost the disciples of Jesus Christ paid.

> ACTS 8:1-3 *"On that day a great persecution broke out against the church in Jerusalem, and all except the apostles were scattered throughout Judea and Samaria. Godly men buried Stephen and mourned deeply for him. But Saul began to destroy the church. Going from house to house, he dragged off both men and women and put them in prison."*

The apostle Peter experienced a variety of the trials the Master had told all his disciples about. Peter encourages the church to persevere and remain faithful as disciples of Jesus Christ and reminds them that the Holy Spirit is with them to accompany and comfort them in difficult times.

THE COST OF SERVING

> 1 PETER 4:12-14 *"Dear friends, do not be surprised at the fiery ordeal that has come on you to test you, as though something strange were happening to you. But rejoice inasmuch as you participate in the sufferings of Christ, so that you may be overjoyed when his glory is revealed. If you are insulted because of the name of Christ, you are blessed, for the Spirit of glory and of God rests on you."*

After his conversion, the apostle Paul was warned by Ananias about the cost that he would pay for being a disciple of Jesus Christ.

> ACTS 9:15-16 *"But the Lord said to Ananias, "Go! This man is my chosen instrument to proclaim my name to the Gentiles and their kings and to the people of Israel. I will show him how much he must suffer for my name."*

Throughout history, the church has built an innumerable cloud of disciples of Jesus Christ, those faithful witnesses who have given their lives in his service. This cloud of heroes of the faith lived and continue to live in accordance with the teachings of the exemplary life of the Master. The biographies of these faithful disciples testify that they lived in the likeness of Christ and some of them paid the high cost of martyrdom for their faith in Jesus. Others have chosen to live without the material amenities, powers, and pleasures that the world offers. They have paid the price of suffering, persecution, imprisonment, torture, rejection, going to unknown countries, and living under constraints of all kinds in the fulfillment of the mission.

> Jesus always spoke of the cost of discipleship and its priority in a life of service (Luke 9:23; 14:25-27, 33). Discipleship is costly, ... but as it is every time that we are to obey God, it will always be more expensive to disobey in the long run. By contrast, to

obey (to be a disciple) is a vigorous investment that ... will spill over into an incomparable source of vitality for the church. It costs, but it is worth it![1]

QUESTIONS FOR REFLECTION

1. How has this chapter about the high cost that Jesus paid in the fulfillment of the mission impacted you?
2. What have you learned about Jesus' teachings of the cost of being his disciple?
3. What other biblical passages would you use for this chapter?
4. Have you been inspired by the cost the apostles paid in the fulfillment of the mission? How?
5. On a scale of 1 to 10, with 10 being the highest score, answer this question: Are you prepared to count the cost for the fulfillment of the mission?

> JEREMIAH 1:8-10 *"'Do not be afraid of them, for I am with you and will rescue you,' declares the Lord. Then the Lord reached out his hand and touched my mouth and said to me, 'I have put my words in your mouth. See, today I appoint you over nations and kingdoms to uproot and tear down, to destroy and overthrow, to build and to plant.'"*

6. How can I persevere in the trials and the cost of being a disciple of Jesus?

> *So I'll cherish the old rugged cross,*
> *Till my trophies at last I lay down.*
> *I will cling to the old rugged cross.*
> *And exchange it someday for a crown.*
>
> —*Sing to the Lord #233*

7. For further reflection on this chapter, if possible, take time to pray and study the scriptures you have found.

CHAPTER 15

KINGDOM FRUIT

"

I am the true vine, and my Father is the gardener. He cuts off every branch in me that bears no fruit, while every branch that does bear fruit he prunes so that it will be even more fruitful. (John 15:1-2)

"

Jesus' miracles reveal the signs of the Kingdom, such as when he turned water into wine so fine that even the master of ceremonies was impressed. In the miracle of catching fish, prior to calling Simon Peter to be a fisher of men, the men caught such a large number of fish the boat became too heavy. Upon feeding the multitudes with just a few loaves of bread and fish, they ended up with 12 extra baskets full of food, even after everyone had eaten their fill.

Jesus taught about the principle of bearing fruit in the fulfillment of the mission with the illustration of the vine. It was a practical example, one that his listeners could understand, to explain the phenomenon of how one, small plant produces so much fruit. Jesus wanted to make sure that his followers had a clear understanding about the importance of producing fruit in the Kingdom.

> The vine is a prolific plant; a single vine produces many grapes. In the Old Testament, grapes symbolized the ability of Israel to bear fruit doing the work of God in the land (Psalms 80:8; Isaiah 5:1-7; Ezekiel 19:10-14).[1]

Jesus emphasized to his disciples what was essential in producing fruit, JOHN 15:8 *"When you produce much fruit, you are my true disciples. This brings great glory to my Father."* The Father expects Jesus' disciples to produce fruit and their lives must be characterized by the fruit of the Kingdom that is *"in keeping with repentance."* Disciples must be known by the type of fruit they produce in their lives and ministries.

In the parable of the sower, Jesus uses an analogy of not taking for granted the importance of producing fruit that is abundant and lasting, MATTHEW 13:8 *"Still other seed fell on good soil, where it produced a crop—a hundred, sixty or thirty times what was sown."* Jesus cursed the fig tree because it only had the appearance of fruit, MATTHEW 21:18-19 *"Early in the morning, as Jesus was on his way back to the city, he was hungry. Seeing a fig tree by the road, he went up to it but found nothing on it except leaves. Then he said to it, 'May you never bear fruit again!' Immediately the tree withered."* Jesus taught another parable to accentuate the importance of producing fruit in the Kingdom. This parable illustrates that those who serve in the Kingdom must bear fruit from the spiritual gifts that are given:

> MATTHEW 25:14-18 *"Again, it will be like a man going on a journey, who called his servants and entrusted his wealth to them. To one he gave five bags of gold, to another two bags, and to another one bag, each according to his ability. Then he went on his journey. The man who had received five bags of gold went at once and put his money to work and gained five bags more. So also, the one with two bags of gold gained two more. But the man who had received one bag went off, dug a hole in the ground and hid his master's money."*

It is clear that Jesus modeled and taught that the Kingdom of God consists of producing fruit in keeping with repentance and the fruit of labor in the work of the mission. The apostles' lives and teachings also speak of the importance of bearing fruit for the Kingdom. The apostle Paul prays that the Colossians bear fruit.

> COLOSSIANS 1:9-10 *"For this reason, since the day we heard about you, we have not stopped praying for you. We continually ask God to fill you with the knowledge of his will through all the wisdom and understanding that the Spirit gives, so that you may live a life worthy of the Lord and please him in every way: bearing fruit in every good work, growing in the knowledge of God."*

Paul also speaks about the gospel of producing fruit when it touches people's lives.

> COLOSSIANS 1:5-6 *"… the true message of the gospel that has come to you. In the same way, the gospel is bearing fruit and growing throughout the whole world—just as it has been doing among you since the day you heard it and truly understood God's grace."*

The apostle Peter writes about the importance of bearing fruit and mentions a series of virtues as fruit.

> 2 PETER 1:8 *"For if you possess these qualities in increasing measure, they will keep you from being ineffective and unproductive in your knowledge of our Lord Jesus Christ."*

The servants of God who have lived under the principle of producing fruit have left their legacies in the lives of the people who have been impacted by their fruitful ministries. The communities where they have served testify to the fruit of the Kingdom. "Each person must seek … the absolute and abundant life that God created for us to experience in Christ."[2]

> What does it mean to be fruitful? The word fruit or some variation of the same is used 55 times in the New Testament and refers to results.[3]

QUESTIONS FOR REFLECTION

1. How has this chapter about producing fruit in the fulfillment of the mission impacted you?
2. How have Jesus' teachings about what is essential for producing fruit in the Kingdom of God helped you?
3. What other biblical passages would you use for this chapter?
4. How have you been inspired by the apostles' teachings of producing fruit in the fulfillment of the mission? How?

5. On a scale of 1 to 10, with 10 being the highest score, answer this question: How much fruit are you producing in the fulfillment of the mission?

   GENESIS 12:1-2 *"The Lord had said to Abram, 'Go from your country, your people and your father's household to the land I will show you. I will make you into a great nation, and I will bless you; I will make your name great, and you will be a blessing.'"*

6. How can I have a fruitful life for the fulfillment of the mission?

   There is joy, joy, Joy in serving Jesus,
   Joy that throbs within my heart;
   Every moment, every hour, As I draw upon His pow'r,
   There is joy, joy, Joy that never shall depart.
   —*"Joy in Serving Jesus," hymnary.org*

7. For further reflection on this chapter, if possible, take time to pray and study the scriptures you have found.

CHAPTER 16

THE MISSION COMMANDMENT

>
> *Then Jesus came to them and said, "All authority in heaven and on earth has been given to me. Therefore go and make disciples of all nations, baptizing them in the name of the Father and of the Son and of the Holy Spirit, and teaching them to obey everything I have commanded you. And surely I am with you always, to the very end of the age."* (Matthew 28:18-20)
>

Jesus became human to carry out the mission of the Father. He devoted his life in total obedience to the mission of the Kingdom. He was clear about the purpose for which the Father had sent him and nothing caused him to deviate from the mission to redeem the human race. Even when he was confronted by the power of darkness in the desert he was not moved, and he resisted all temptations that confronted him.

> Hebrews 4:14-15 *"Therefore, since we have a great high priest who has ascended into heaven, Jesus the Son of God, let us hold firmly to the faith we profess. For we do not have a high priest who is unable to empathize with our weaknesses, but we have one who has been tempted in every way, just as we are—yet he did not sin."*

Jesus assured his disciples that he had all authority in heaven and on earth and, therefore, sent them to fulfill the mission of the Kingdom. The apostle Peter was witness to that reality and writes about it to the church.

> 2 Peter 3:21-22 *"By the resurrection of Jesus Christ, who has gone into heaven and is at God's right hand— with angels, authorities and powers in submission to him."*

Jesus established and taught his disciples the principles and values that would govern his church as it fulfilled the mission. He spent three years of his life shaping his team of disciples so they would go on to do the same and carry on the mission of the Kingdom. Now the mission would be in the immediate hands of his disciples under the direction and power of the Holy Spirit. It was up to these fishermen, tax collectors, church leaders, and all who embraced citizenship of the new Kingdom to continue the mission of the Kingdom of God.

The victorious Christ empowered them with his authority and with the power of the Holy Spirit and gave them specific instructions about what to do and what to teach to carry out the mission. The driving force of the mission was to go and teach the principles and values that Jesus had taught them about the Kingdom. An essential part of the mission was making new disciples of Jesus Christ so they, in turn, would go and bring the message of the good news of the Kingdom.

> Jesus' plan of discipleship is multiplication. Every disciple must disciple another. This is evident in the way that Jesus sent his disciples to preach in pairs and in his final commission.[1]

The Great Commission is the commandment for proclaiming and advancing the gospel. The church has no greater objective than to fulfill the imperative to "go" and make disciples of all nations on earth.

> The Great Commission, announced by Jesus in Matthew 28:19-20, is God's invitation to be part of the greatest project in history. … A (pastor or leader) believer or a church that is committed to the Great Commission will experience the power to be different and make a difference in the world.[2]

Before his ascension to be at the right hand of the Father, Jesus reminded the disciples over and over about the mission.

> LUKE 24:46-48 *"He told them, 'This is what is written: The Messiah will suffer and rise from the dead on the third day, and repentance for the forgiveness of sins will be preached in his name to all nations, beginning at Jerusalem. You are witnesses of these things.'"*

The early church fulfilled the commandment to share the good news of the Kingdom. When it was necessary to take the gospel outside of Jerusalem, the apostles sent Peter and John to check on and confirm the new believers in the region of

Samaria. ᴀᴄᴛs 8:15-16 *"When they arrived, they prayed for the new believers there that they might receive the Holy Spirit, because the Holy Spirit had not yet come on any of them; they had simply been baptized in the name of the Lord Jesus."* After seeing how the people of Samaria received the good news of Jesus Christ, Peter and John went home. ᴀᴄᴛs 8:25 *"After they had further proclaimed the word of the Lord and testified about Jesus, Peter and John returned to Jerusalem, preaching the gospel in many Samaritan villages."*

The apostle Paul was obedient to the commission of Jesus Christ to take the message to the Gentiles, and he devoted his life to preaching the gospel.

> ʀᴏᴍᴀɴs 15:20-21 *"It has always been my ambition to preach the gospel where Christ was not known, so that I would not be building on someone else's foundation. Rather, as it is written: 'Those who were not told about him will see, and those who have not heard will understand.'"*

The church has been commissioned to carry out the mission of the Kingdom of God for the redemption of the human race through the merits of the Son, Jesus Christ. The mission of God depends on the faithful obedience of the church to share the message of God's love and salvation for all people.

> We are a sent people, responding to the call of Christ and empowered by the Holy Spirit to go into all the world, witnessing to the lordship of Christ and participating with God in the building of the church and the extension of his Kingdom (2 Corinthians 6:1).[3]

The men and women called to fulfill the mission of the church have a full understanding of the commandment and commission of Jesus Christ to go into the whole world evangelizing and making disciples. It is essential to make disciples of Jesus for the establishment and extension of the Kingdom of God in the hearts of people, and hence, in the overall transformation of their communities.

> Discipleship and evangelism are inseparable. In reality, they are the same thing. We are called to keep in constant contact with unbelievers in order to witness to them and win them for Christ. God's plan to redeem the world is dependent on each one of us to win others to Christ.[4]

QUESTIONS FOR REFLECTION

1. How has this chapter about Jesus' commandment to his disciples impacted you?
2. How have Jesus' teachings about the mission of the Kingdom of God helped you?
3. What other biblical passages would you use for this chapter?
4. Have you been inspired by the apostles dedication to fulfill the mission under the power and guidance of the Holy Spirit? How?
5. On a scale of 1 to 10, with 10 being the highest score, answer this question: Am I fulfilling the church's mission?

> EXODUS 3:7-10 *"The Lord said, 'I have indeed seen the misery of my people in Egypt. I have heard them crying out because of their slave drivers, and I am concerned about their suffering. So I have come down to rescue them from the hand of the Egyptians and to bring them up out of that land into a good and spacious land, a land flowing with milk and honey ... and I have seen the way the Egyptians*

> *are oppressing them. So now, go. I am sending you to Pharaoh to bring my people the Israelites out of Egypt.'"*

6. How can I carry out the mission of the church?

> *In the beauty of the lilies*
> *Christ was born across the sea,*
> *With a glory in His bosom*
> *that transfigures you and me:*
> *As He died to make men holy,*
> *let us live to make men free,*
> *While God is marching on.*

> —*Sing to the Lord #756*

7. For further reflection on this chapter, if possible, take time to pray and study the scriptures you have found.

CONCLUSION

In the Gospels we find stories from Jesus' life as he fulfilled the mission of the Kingdom of God. He empowered and trained his disciples with the essential values and principles of the Kingdom. Jesus knew that carrying on the mission of the church would fall to the faithful obedience of his disciples under the direction and the anointing power of the Holy Spirit.

The disciples learned the teachings from the Master and followed his footsteps in guiding the early church in the fulfillment of the mission. The principles they received from the Master, such as a life of total dependence on and relationship with the Father, a life full of the power of the Holy Spirit, the use of the Scriptures, prayer and fasting, proclaiming the gospel, intentional discipleship, compassion, organization, producing fruit, and the high cost of serving with the sacrifice of their lives were the key elements with which the gospel of Jesus Christ was established and grew exponentially in the first century and afterwards. The apostles lived the principles and teachings that Jesus taught, and then they taught these principles to the church. The apostle Paul dared to say, 1 CORINTHIANS 11:1 *"Follow my example, as I follow the example of Christ."*

FULFILLING THE MISSION

The writings of the New Testament, the historical documents of the church, and the biographies of the servants of God testify to how the church has been fulfilling the Greatest Commandment and the Great Commission of Jesus Christ. The new cloud of witnesses faithful to the call of God have followed the steps, principles of the life and teachings of the Master in obedience, dedication, passion, and sacrifice guided by the power of the Holy Spirit in the fulfillment of the mission. They inspire us with their lives and tell us that it is possible to live the principles that Jesus lived and taught to his disciples to establish and advance the Kingdom of God. It is my prayer that these reflections on Jesus' principles have blessed, helped, and challenged you to apply them to your ministry in *fulfilling the mission* of the church:

"MAKE CHRISTLIKE DISCIPLES IN THE NATIONS"

NOTES

CHAPTER 1
1. H. Orton Wiley and Paul T. Culbertson, *Introduction to Christian Theology,* 1948, Spanish edition, 184.
2. *Biblia del diario vivir*. Nashville: Editorial Caribe, 2000, Electronic editions, Gen 3:15.
3. Wiley and Culbertson, 209.

CHAPTER 2
1. *Biblia del diario vivir,* Luke 2:43.
2. Wiley and Culbertson, 278.
3. Wesley L. Duewel, *Ablaze for God*, 1995, Spanish edition. 51.
4. *Nazarene Essentials,* Kansas City: Church of the Nazarene, 2015.
5. Carl Bangs, *Phineas E. Bresee: Pastor to the People.*
6. Duewel, 48.

CHAPTER 3
1. *Biblia del diario vivir,* Luke 4:16.
2. *Manual Church of the Nazarene, 2013-2017.*
3. *Biblia del diario vivir,* Luke 4:16

CHAPTER 4

1. *Biblia del diario vivir,* Luke 2:43
2. Watchman Nee, *Spiritual Authority*, 1990 Spanish edition, 47.
3. J. W. Hayford, *The Spirit-Filled Family: Holy Wisdom to Build Happy Homes*, Nashville: Editorial Caribe, 1995, Spanish edition, 90.

CHAPTER 5

1. *Biblia del diario vivir,* Matthew 6:9.
2. Duewel, 66.
3. Duewel, 76.
4. Duewel, 251.
5. Duewel, 236.

CHAPTER 6

1. Diego Forero, *La hoja de ruta,* Lenexa, KS: Casa Nazarena de publicaciones, 2016, 6.
2. Gene Mims, *The Kingdom Focused Church,* Spanish edition, 77.

CHAPTER 7

1. W. M. Nelson and J. R. Mayo, *Nelson's New Illustrated Bible Dictionary*, Nashville: Editorial Caribe, electronic edition, 1998.
2. Nelson and Mayo.
3. Nelson and Mayo
4. Duewel, 54-55.

CHAPTER 8

1. Nelson and Mayo
2. Mims, 49.

NOTES

3. Mims, 14.

CHAPTER 9
1. Hayford, J. W., *Power Faith: Balancing Faith in Words and Works,*. Nashville: Editorial Caribe, 2000, electronic edition, 5.

CHAPTER 10
1. David L. McKenna, *Wesleyanos en el siglo XXI,* 80.
2. Floyd Cunningham, *Our Watchword & Song.* Spanish edition,234.
3. *Nazarene Essentials.*
4. *http://www.usacanadaregion.org/mission-and-vision*

CHAPTER 11
1. Luciano Jaramillo, *Jesús ejecutivo,* 13.
2. Jaramillo, 123.

CHAPTER 12
1. Horace G. Cowan, *The Sabbath in Scripture and History,* Spanish edition, 12.
2. Daniel Spaite, *Time Bomb in the Church,* Spanish edition, 125.
3. Spaite, 127.

CHAPTER 13
1. Rick Warren, *The Purpose Driven Church,* Spanish edition, p. 216.
2. *Biblia del diario vivir,* Gn 3.15
3. John C. Bowling, *Grace – Full Leadership,* Spanish edition, 14.

CHAPTER 14

1. Luis Aranguren and Fabián D. Ruiz, *Ministerio discipular*, 26.

CHAPTER 15

1. *Biblia del diario vivir,* Gn 3.15).
2. Mims, ix.
3. Warren, 70.

CHAPTER 16

1. Aranguren and Ruiz, 16.
2. Aranguren and Ruiz, 4.
3. *Nazarene Essentials.*
4. Mims, 92.

www.ingramcontent.com/pod-product-compliance
Lightning Source LLC
Chambersburg PA
CBHW031447040426
42444CB00007B/1008